THIRD EDITION

ACTIVE

SKILLS FOR READING: Intro

Neil J Anderson

NATIONAL GEOGRAPHIC LEARNING

HEINLE CENGAGE Learning

Australia • Brazil • Japan • Korea • Mexico • Singapore • Spain • United Kingdom • United States

Active Skills for Reading Intro, Third Edition

Neil J Anderson

Publisher, Asia and Global ELT:
  Andrew Robinson

Senior Development Editor: Derek Mackrell

Associate Development Editor: Claire Tan

Director of Global Marketing: Ian Martin

Academic Marketing Manager:
  Emily Stewart

Marketing Communications Manager:
  Beth Leonard

Director of Content and Media Production:
  Michael Burggren

Associate Content Project Manager:
  Mark Rzeszutek

Manufacturing Manager: Marcia Locke

Manufacturing Planner:
  Mary Beth Hennebury

Composition: PreMediaGlobal

Cover Design: Page2, LLC

For product information and technology assistance, contact us at
Cengage Learning Customer & Sales Support, 1-800-354-9706

For permission to use material from this text or product, submit all requests online at **cengage.com/permissions**
Further permissions questions can be emailed to
permissionrequest@cengage.com

Library of Congress Control Number: 2007922480

ISBN-13: 978-1-133-30812-6
ISBN-10: 1-133-30812-0

National Geographic Learning
20 Channel Center Street
Boston, MA 02210
USA

Cengage Learning is a leading provider of customized learning solutions with office locations around the globe, including Singapore, the United Kingdom, Australia, Mexico, Brazil, and Japan.

Cengage Learning products are represented in Canada by Nelson Education, Ltd.

Visit National Geographic Learning online at **elt.heinle.com**
Visit our corporate website at **www.cengage.com**

Photo credits
FRONT MATTER: Thinkstock: Hemera/Getty Images, Jupiterimages/Getty Images, Jupiterimages/Getty Images, Hemera/Getty Images; **p11:** Dreamstime: Monkeybusinessimages (tr), Yuri_acrurs (tl), Pradi (cr); Shutterstock: Stephen Coburn (cl), Photosani (c); **p13:** Shutterstock: Photosani, Ersler Dmitry (tr), Peter Kirillov (cr), Andresr (r), Anton Albert (bc), Alen (b); Dreamstime: Leaf (bc), Delamofoto (bc), Nejron (br), Diego.Cervo. (b); **p17:** Photos.com (tr); Shutterstock: chrisbrignell (bl); **p21:** Dreamstime: Andresr (tl), Michaeljung (tr), Fotosmurf02 (cl), Astargirl (cr); Photos.com: JupiterImages (c); **p23:** Dreamstime: Avava (r), Tonylivingstone (r); **p25:** Photos.com: JupiterImages/Brand X Pictures/Getty Images/Thinkstock; **p27:** Shutterstock: Andresr (tr); Photos.com: Photos.com (r); Dreamstime: Vgstudio (cr), Goodynewshoes (cr), Ariwasabi (br); **p31:** Thinkstock: Digital Vison (tl), George Doyle (cl); Dreamstime: Dynamitecreative (tr), Pressmaster (cr); Shutterstock: Monkey Business Images (c); **p33:** OneWeekJob: Ian MacKenzie (t); Shutterstock: Gary Paul Lewis (r); **p37:** Shutterstock: Lledo (r); Peter Kirillov (cr); Getty Images: Ian Cook/Time Life Pictures (tr), Timothy A. Clary (cl); **p40:** iStockphoto: Mie Ahmt (tr); **p49:** Thinkstock: Ryan McVay/Digital Vison (tl), BananaStock (r), JupiterImages/Brand X Pictures (cl), Hemera (cr); **p53:** Shutterstock: Tungphoto, Alistair Michael Thomas (tr); **p55:** Thinkstock: Brand X Pictures (tr), Hemera (cl, l, bl); **p59:** iStockphoto: chris_lemmens; **p61:** Thinkstock: Stockbyte (t), Dynamic Graphics/liquidlibrary (cr); **p65:** Shutterstock: Edwin Verin (br), joyfull (tc); **p68:** Shutterstock: Malchev (t), Emjay Smith (cr); **p69:** Thinkstock: Ryan McVay/Photodisc (tl), iStockphoto (tr); **p71:** iStockphoto: hipokrat (tr); Shutterstock: BlueOrange Studio (br); **p75:** Thinkstock: Hemera (tr), Comstock/Getty Images (br); Shutterstock: Morgan Lane Photography (cr); **p87:** Thinkstock: istockphoto (tc), Hemera (c), Goodshoot/Jupiterimages/GettyImages (cr), Comstock (bc), Shutterstock: Monkey Business Images (cl), ejwhite (cl); iStockphoto: Sean Locke (bc); **p88:** Shutterstock: Anton Gvozdikov (r); **p89:** Thinkstock: Siri Stafford; **p93:** Thinkstock: iStockphoto (tr); **p96:** Thinkstock: Hemera (cl); Dreamstime: Pinkcandy (c); Shutterstock: James Steidl (cr), Anya Ponti (br), Morozova Oxana (bc), oliveromg (br); **p97:** Shutterstock: Natursports (tl), Peter Kirillov (cr); Getty Images: Ian Cook/Time Life Pictures (tr), Timothy A. Clary (cl); **p98:** Thinkstock: Hemera; **p99:** Shutterstock: kojoku (tr); Getty Images: Mustafa Ozer/AFP (t); **p103:** Lonely Planet: Lou Jones (tr); Shutterstock: sunsetman (cr); **p107:** Shutterstock: Helga Esteb (tl), stocklight (tr), Featureflash (cl, cr); **p109:** Shutterstock: Gustavo Miguel Fernandes (tc), DFree (tr); **p112:** Thinkstock: istockphoto (c, cl); Shutterstock: Ayakovlev.com (cr, c); **p113:** Getty Images: Timothy A. Clary/AFP (t,b); **p125:** Thinkstock: Goodshoot (tl), Photodisc (tc,tr), istockphoto (bl, br, tr); **p127:** Shutterstock: Andrey Arkusha (r); Thinkstock: lifesize (l); **p131:** Getty Images: Miguel Benitez (tr); Photos.com: Grata Victoria (c); Shutterstock: Africa Studio (tc), djem(tr), Tyler Olson (c), Mike Flippo (cr), Natalia Aggiato; **p135:** Thinkstock: Comstock (tl); Shutterstock: corepics (cl), lIghtpoet (bc), Peter Kim (tr); **p137:** Creative Commons (cr, c, br); **p141:** Federal Bureau of Investigation (tr); **p145:** Shutterstock: Supri Suharjoto (tl); Thinkstock: Stockbyte (tr); iStockPhoto: pressureUA (bl), Peeter Viisimaa (br); **p147:** Jesus Morales (tr); Thinkstock: Todd Warnock (cr); **p151:** AP Photo: Chilean Government, Hugo Infante (tr); Newscom: Cezaro De Luca (cl); Getty Images: Martin Bernetti (br); **p42:** Thinkstock: Hemera (tr), Jupiterimages/Brand X Pictures (bl); **p45:** Thinkstock: Hemera (cr); **p47:** Thinkstock: Hemera Technologies/AbleStock.com (r), Comstock (c), iStockphoto (r,l), Jupiterimages/Photos.com (c), Jetta Productions/Lifesize (c), George Doyle & Ciaran Griffin (l); **p80:** Thinkstock: iStockphoto (tr, l, bl), Hemera (cr); **p83:** Thinkstock: iStockphoto (tr); Getty Images: Getty Images Sport (bl); Shutterstock: Vahe Katrjyan (cr); **p85:** Newscom: Jameson Wu/EyePress News EyePress (r); Getty Images: Daniel Acker/Bloomberg (l); **p118:** Shutterstock: Dmitry Vinogradov (tr); Thinkstock: iStockphoto (br); **p121:** AP Photo: Ted S. Warren (l); **p123:** Shutterstock: Entertainment Press (t); **p156:** AP Photo: David X Prutting/BFAnyc/Sipa Press (r); **p159:** Getty Images: Alexander Tamargo; Shutterstock: Erik Lam; **p161:** Press Association Images: Tim Ockenden/PA Archive (r); Getty Images: Mike Hewitt (l).

Printed in Canada
3 4 5 6 7 17 16 15 14

Dedication & Acknowledgments

This book is dedicated to the students and teachers who have used *ACTIVE Skills for Reading* over the past ten years. Since 2002/2003 when the first edition of *ACTIVE Skills for Reading* was published, thousands of students and teachers have used the book. I know that I had no idea that the series would be this popular and that we would reach the stage of publishing a third edition.

The pedagogical framework for this series is as viable today as it has ever been. As students and teachers use each of the elements of *ACTIVE*, stronger reading will result.

My associations with the editorial team in Singapore continue to be some of my greatest professional relationships. I express appreciation to Sean Bermingham, Derek Mackrell, and Andrew Robinson for their commitment to excellence in publishing. I also express appreciation to Jenny Wilsen and John Murn for their commitment to helping the third edition be stronger than the two previous editions.

Neil J Anderson

Reviewers for this edition

Mardelle Azimi; **Jose Carmona** Hillsborough Community College; **Grace Chao** Soochow University; **Mei-Rong Alice Chen** National Taiwan University of Science and Technology; **Irene Dryden; Jennifer Farnell** Greenwich Japanese School; **Kathy Flynn** Glendale Community College; **Sandy Hartmann** University of Houston; **Joselle L. LaGuerre; Margaret V. Layton; Myra M. Medina** Miami Dade College; **Masumi Narita** Tokyo International University; **Margaret Shippey** Miami Dade College; **Satoshi Shiraki; Karen Shock** Savannah College of Art and Design; **Sandrine Ting; Colin S. Ward** Lonestar College; **Virginia West** Texas A&M University; **James B. Wilson; Ming-Nuan Yang** Chang Gung Institute of Technology; **Jakchai Yimngam** Rajamangala University of Technology

Reviewers of the second edition

Chiou-lan Chern National Taiwan Normal University; **Cheongsook Chin** English Campus Institute, Inje University; **Yang Hyun** Jung-Ang Girls' High School; **Li Junhe** Beijing No.4 High School; **Tim Knight** Gakushuin Women's College; **Ahmed M. Motala** University of Sharjah; **Gleides Ander Nonato** Colégio Arnaldo and Centro Universitário Newton Paiva; **Ethel Ogane** Tamagawa University; **Seung Ku Park** Sunmoon University; **Shu-chien, Sophia, Pan** College of Liberal Education, Shu-Te University; **Marlene Tavares de Allmeida** Wordshop Escola de Linguas; **Naowarat Tongkam** Silpakorn University; **Nobuo Tsuda** Konan University; **Hasan Hüseyin Zeyrek** Istanbul Kültür University Faculty of Economics and Administrative Sciences

Contents

Vocabulary Learning Tips

Learning new vocabulary is an important part of learning to be a good reader. Remember that the letter **C** in **ACTIVE Skills for Reading** reminds us to cultivate vocabulary.

1 Decide if the word is worth learning now

As you read you will find many words you do not know. You will slow your reading fluency if you stop at every new word. For example, you should stop to find out the meaning of a new word if:
  - **a.** you read the same word many times.
  - **b.** the word appears in the heading of a passage, or in the topic sentence of a paragraph—the sentence that gives the main idea of the paragraph.

2 Record information about new words you decide to learn

Keep a vocabulary notebook in which you write words you want to remember. Complete the following information for words that you think are important to learn:

New word	collect
Translation	收集
Part of speech	verb
Sentence where found	Jamie Oliver collected more than 270,000 signatures from people.
My own sentence	My brother collects stamps.

3 Learn words from the same family

For many important words in English that you will want to learn, the word is part of a word family. As you learn new words, learn words in the family from other parts of speech (nouns, verbs, adjectives, adverbs, etc.).

Noun	happiness
Verb	
Adjective	happy
Adverb	happily

4 Learn words that go with the key word you are learning

When we learn new words, it is important to learn what other words are frequently used with them. These are called collocations. Here is an example from a student's notebook.

take		long		next week
go on	a	two-week	vacation	in Italy
need		short		with my family
have		summer		by myself
		school		

5 *Create a word web*

A word web is a picture that helps you connect words together and helps you increase your vocabulary. Here is a word web for the word "frightened":

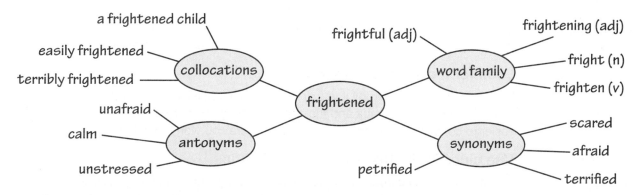

6 *Memorize common prefixes, roots, and suffixes*

Many English words can be divided into different parts. We call these parts *prefixes*, *roots*, and *suffixes*. A *prefix* comes at the beginning of a word, a *suffix* comes at the end of a word, and the *root* is the main part of the word. In your vocabulary notebook, make a list of prefixes and suffixes as you come across them. On page 175 there is a list of prefixes and suffixes in this book. For example, look at the word "unhappily."

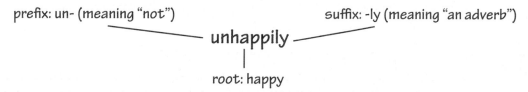

7 *Regularly review your vocabulary notebook*

You should review the words in your vocabulary notebook very often. The more often you review your list of new words, the sooner you will be able to recognize the words when you see them during reading. Set up a schedule to go over the words you are learning.

8 *Make vocabulary flash cards*

Flash cards are easy to make, and you can carry them everywhere with you. You can use them to study while you are waiting for the bus, walking to school or work, or eating a meal. You can use the flash cards with your friends to quiz each other. Here is an example of a flash card:

Front   Back

Tips for Fluent Reading

Find time to read every day.

Find the best time of day for you to read. Try to read when you are not tired. By reading every day, even for a short period, you will become a more fluent reader.

Look for a good place to read.

It is easier to read and study if you are comfortable. Make sure that there is good lighting in your reading area and that you are sitting in a comfortable chair. To make it easier to concentrate, try to read in a place where you won't be interrupted.

Use clues in the text to make predictions.

Fluent readers make predictions before and as they read. Use the title, subtitle, pictures, and captions to ask yourself questions about what you are going to read. Find answers to the questions when you read. After reading, think about what you have learned and decide what you need to read next to continue learning.

Establish goals before you read.

Before you read a text, think about the purpose of your reading. For example, do you just want to get a general idea of the passage? Or do you need to find specific information? Thinking about what you want to get from the reading will help you decide what reading skills you need to use.

Notice how your eyes and head are moving.

Good readers use their eyes, and not their heads, when they read. Moving your head back and forth when reading will make you tired. Practice avoiding head movements by placing your elbows on the table and resting your head in your hands. Do you feel movement as you read? If you do, hold your head still as you read. Also, try not to move your eyes back over a text. You should reread part of a text only when you have a specific purpose for rereading, for example, to make a connection between what you read previously and what you are reading now.

Try not to translate.

Translation slows down your reading. Instead of translating new words into your first language, first try to guess the meaning. Use the context (the other words around the new word) and word parts (prefixes, suffixes, and word roots) to help you guess the meaning.

Read in phrases rather than word by word.

Don't point at each word while you read. Practice reading in phrases—groups of words that go together.

Engage your imagination.

Good readers visualize what they are reading. They create a movie in their head of the story they are reading. As you read, try sharing with a partner the kinds of pictures that you create in your mind.

Avoid subvocalization.

Subvocalization means quietly saying the words as you read. You might be whispering the words or just silently saying them in your mind. Your eyes and brain can read much faster than you can speak. If you subvocalize, you can only read as fast as you can say the words. As you read, place your finger on your lips or your throat. Do you feel movement? If so, you are subvocalizing. Practice reading without moving your lips.

Don't worry about understanding every word.

Sometimes, as readers, we think we must understand the meaning of everything that we read. It isn't always necessary to understand every word in a passage in order to understand the meaning of the passage as a whole. Instead of interrupting your reading to find the meaning of a new word, circle the word and come back to it after you have finished reading.

Enjoy your reading.

Your enjoyment of reading will develop over time. Perhaps today you do not like to read in English, but as you read more, you should see a change in your attitude. The more you read in English, the easier it will become. You will find yourself looking forward to reading.

Read as much as you can.

The best tip to follow to become a more fluent reader is to read whenever and wherever you can. Good readers read a lot. They read many different kinds of material: newspapers, magazines, textbooks, websites, and graded readers. To practice this, keep a reading journal. Every day, make a list of the kinds of things you read during the day and how long you read each for. If you want to become a more fluent reader, read more!

Are You an ACTIVE Reader?

Before you use this book to develop your reading skills, think about your reading habits, and your strengths and weaknesses when reading in English. Check the statements that are true for you.

		Start of course	End of course
1	I read something in English every day.	☐	☐
2	I try to read where I'm comfortable and won't be interrupted.	☐	☐
3	I make predictions about what I'm going to read before I start reading.	☐	☐
4	I think about my purpose of reading before I start reading.	☐	☐
5	I keep my head still, and move only my eyes, when I read.	☐	☐
6	I try not to translate words from English to my first language.	☐	☐
7	I read in phrases rather than word by word.	☐	☐
8	I try to picture in my mind what I'm reading.	☐	☐
9	I read silently, without moving my lips.	☐	☐
10	I try to understand the meaning of the passage, and try not to worry about understanding the meaning of every word.	☐	☐
11	I usually enjoy reading in English.	☐	☐
12	I try to read as much as I can, especially outside class.	☐	☐

Follow the tips on pages 8–9. These will help you become a more active reader. At the end of the course, answer this quiz again to see if you have become a more fluent, active reader.

Getting Ready

A **Match the words in the box with the pictures above.**

> **a.** a computer   **d.** a website
> **b.** a video game   **e.** a cell phone
> **c.** an e-reader

B **Answer these questions. (Circle) yes or no. Discuss your answers with a partner.**

1	I have a computer.	Yes	No
2	I have my own website or blog.	Yes	No
3	I read books on an e-reader.	Yes	No
4	I spend a lot of time online.	Yes	No
5	I read books on my cell phone.	Yes	No
6	I text message my friends.	Yes	No
7	I like to play video or computer games.	Yes	No

CHAPTER 1 Meeting Friends Online

Before You Read
My Friends

A Think about answers to these questions.

  1 What **social networks** (e.g. *Facebook*) do you use? How many online friends do you have?

  2 How often do you meet your friends? What do you do?

B Discuss your answers with a partner.

Reading Skill
Scanning

> You *scan* to find information fast. You don't read every word. People often scan a website, a schedule, or a phone book for specific information.

A Look at the website on the next page for five seconds. Then read the sentences in the chart below. Do you think the answers are true or false? Check (✓) true (T) or false (F).

		T	F
1	On Face2Face, I can meet my friends online.	✓	
2	On Face2Face, I can talk about movies.	✓	
3	On Face2Face, I can telephone my friends.		✓
4	On Face2Face, I can make music videos.	✓	✓

B Scan the passage on the next page. Were your answers in **A** correct?

C Read the website on the next page. Then answer the questions on page 14.

> **Reading helps you in the world.** Being a good reader in both your first language and in English is useful to you and your community. You will benefit as a citizen of the world as you read more about events happening in different parts of the world. Your knowledge of the world can help you as a citizen of the community you live in.

Make friends around the world!

Face2Face has six million members worldwide. **Join today.** It's free!

On Face2Face you can . . .

5

- make your own homepage. Put **photos** of yourself and your friends on your page. Tell the world about you: your name and age, your hobbies,[1] your hometown, your school, your **favorite** food, movies, and music.

- meet your friends online. You can also **make friends** with other Face2Face members.

10

- start a blog. Write your thoughts and tell stories online. Read other people's blogs.

- put music and video on your page.

- join or start a **discussion** group. Talk about different topics (movies, music, sports, travel).

15

- **send text messages** from your computer to a friend's cell phone. You can also **leave a message** on a friend's homepage.

- play games alone or with other Face2Face members.

- watch new music videos. Listen to your favorite songs. Read about bands and singers. Learn about shows in your **area**.

20

- read about new movies and your favorite actors. Watch short previews[2] of new movies. **Buy** movie tickets online.

Your profile can look like this . . .

---

[1] A **hobby** is an activity you do in your free time.
[2] A **preview** is a short part of a movie you watch before the movie starts in cinemas.

Reading Comprehension
Check Your Understanding

A Choose the correct answers.

1 How many people use Face2Face?
   a four hundred
   b two thousand
   c six million
2 What CAN'T you do on Face2Face?
   a make your own video
   b join a discussion group
   c make a homepage
3 What is a blog?
   a a place to write your thoughts
   b a website with video games
   c a place to make new friends
4 On Face2Face, you can play games _____.
   a alone
   b with Face2Face members
   c both alone and with other members

B At the top of the Face2Face website, there are eight words (Home, My Page, etc.). Read the sentences below. Which word(s) do you click? Write your answer(s).

		Word(s) to Click
1	Lady Gaga has a new CD. I want to hear her new song.	*Music*
2	I want to change my personal information.	
3	I want to read about other people using Face2Face.	
4	I plan to visit Greece this summer. I want ideas about things to do.	

Critical Thinking

C 1 Do you like the Face2Face website? Why?
   2 Do you know other websites like Face2Face?

Vocabulary Comprehension
Words in Context

A In each sentence, circle the best answer. The words in blue are from the passage.

1 Pedro: "This is a photo of my girlfriend."
   Liz: "What a nice (drawing / picture)!"
2 I really (like / hate) green. It's my favorite color.
3 You can make friends (in a book / on the Internet).
4 In our discussion group, we (talk / read) about different topics.
5 To (send / leave) your text message to Mario, press this button.
6 Tina calls John. John isn't home. She hears his answering machine: "Hi, this is John. I'm not home. Please (send a message / leave a message) after the beep."

7 Fumiko: "You live in a very beautiful area."

Jose: "Yes, I do. My (city / house) is on many postcards."

8 I want to buy a DVD, but I don't have any (money / friends).

B **Answer the questions below. Discuss your answers with a partner.**

1 You can make friends in a club. What is another way?

_____

2 Do you send emails or text messages to your friends? How often?

_____

3 Do you ever buy things online?

_____

4 Do you think you live in a beautiful area? Why or why not?

_____

A **Is each noun singular or plural? Check (✔) the correct answer.**

Noun		singular	plural
1	blog		
2	hobbies		
3	homepage		
4	message		
5	videos		
6	game		
7	movies		
8	members		
9	actor		
10	stories		

Vocabulary Skill
Singular and Plural Nouns

Singular means *one*. Plural means *more than one*. Plural nouns usually end in *-s* or *-es*. For example, *cat* is singular. *Cats* is plural.

B **Complete each sentence with a noun from A. Use the correct singular or plural form.**

1 Johnny Depp is my favorite _____. I have all his

_____ on DVD.

2 There are two _____ on your answering machine.

3 My brother often plays computer _____ with friends.

4 Every day I write on my _____. That way my friends know what I've been doing.

5 Alan is a(n) _____ of a local gym. He exercises a lot.

Before You Read
Let's Play!

A **Think about answers to these questions.**

1 Look at the picture on the next page. What are the people doing?

2 What computer or video games do you know? Do you play them? How often?

3 Read the sentence below. What do you think *active* means?

> As a child, Jason was very active. He was always running around and playing.

B **Discuss your answers with a partner.**

Reading Skill
Predicting from the Title

> Always read the title first. From the title, you can predict (guess) the passage's ideas.

A **Look at the title of the passage on the next page. What do you predict the passage is about? Complete the sentence.**

I think the passage is about _____.

B **Read the whole passage. Then check your answer in A. Were you correct?**

C **Read the passage again. Then answer the questions on page 18.**

ACTIVE Gaming

guitar

On Friday, David went home from college to visit his family. In the living room, David's 14-year-old brother, Jason, was in front of the
5 television. Jason looked **crazy**, jumping around and talking to himself.

"What are you doing?" David asked.

10 "I'm playing *Dance Central*," Jason said. "Want to try?"

There was no controller.[1] Jason told his brother to stand in front of the television. Then Jason
15 said that the **machine** could see and hear them. The machine was also **connected** to the television. If they wanted to, the brothers could tell the machine to **turn off** the game so they
20 can watch TV.

David was ready to play! Jason pointed his finger at the screen and started a two-player music game. In the
25 game they were **rock** musicians, playing guitars and dancing.

Playing the game made David feel **tired**. He had to move his arms, legs, hands, and feet to play the game. Being so 30 active, David felt **like** he was actually in the game, not just controlling it.

It was **terrific**! Before they knew it, they had played **nonstop** for two hours.
Someone once said that 35 technology can seem like magic. Standing in front of the television, David certainly felt like a magician.[2]

[1] A **controller**

[2] A **magician** is someone who does magic.

Reading Comprehension
Check Your Understanding

A **Choose the correct answers.**

1 What was Jason doing at home?
   a He was exercising.
   b He was watching television.
   c He was dancing.

2 Why did David feel tired?
   a He did not get enough sleep last night.
   b He had to move around a lot.
   c He played the game for too long.

3 In line 34, the word **nonstop** means _____.
   a stopping often
   b without stopping
   c for one hour

4 What is special about the video game in this passage?
   a Players do not use controllers.
   b The players learn to play music.
   c The game is played online.

B **Put the events below in order from 1 to 6.**

a _____ David felt tired.
b _____ David came home from college.
c _____ Jason pointed his finger at the screen.
d _____ David felt like a magician.
e _____ David saw Jason jumping around.
f _____ David and Jason played the game.

Critical Thinking

C 1 Are video games without controllers better than video games with controllers? Why?
   2 Do you want to play the video game in the passage? Why?

Vocabulary Comprehension
Definitions

A **Match each word with its definition. The words in blue are from the passage.**

1	like	_d_	a sleepy
2	crazy	_____	b for example: a car, a television
3	machine	_____	c very good
4	connected	_____	d similar to
5	turn off	_____	e strange
6	rock	_____	f together
7	terrific	_____	g to stop using
8	tired	_____	h a kind of loud music

B   Answer the questions below. Discuss your answers with a partner.

1 How many different kinds of machine can you name?

_____

2 What time do you turn off the lights and go to sleep?

_____

3 What makes you tired?

_____

4 Do you look like your mother or your father? How?

_____

A   Add -er or -r to each verb to create a new noun.

	Verb	Noun
1	dance	_____
2	surf	_____
3	write	_____
4	design	_____
5	paint	_____
6	play	_____
7	read	_____
8	speak	_____
9	listen	_____
10	sing	_____

Vocabulary Skill
Adding -er or -r to
Make New Words

In English, we can
add -er to verbs to
make nouns. For
example, play + er =
player. If the noun or
verb ends in e, we only
add an r. For example,
game + r = gamer.

B   Use nouns from A to complete the sentences.

1 Tommy Hilfiger is a famous clothing ____designer____ .

2 Marco is a _____ . He goes to the beach almost every day.

3 Mia talks too much. She needs to be a better _____ .

4 Picasso and Monet are famous _____ .

5 Wei Ping is a good _____ . Have you read any of her stories?

C   Do you know other words like the ones in A? Make a list. Compare your list with a partner's.

Review your performance. Review your answers to all of the reading comprehension and vocabulary comprehension exercises in this unit. If you got any of the items incorrect, why do you think you did?

Real Life Skill
Starting a Blog in English

You can use a blog to practice reading and writing in English.

A Carlos has a blog. Read his profile. Then complete your profile.

Carlos's Profile

First name: Carlos

Last name: Alvarez

Email address:
carlito@blog.heinle.com

User name: CarlosA

Birthday: June 23, 1989

Gender: [X] Male [ ] Female

City: Valencia

Country: Spain

Name of my blog:
What's up, Carlito?

Your Profile

First name:

Last name:

Email address:

User name:

Birthday:

Gender: [ ] Male [ ] Female

City:

Country:

Name of my blog:

B Go to one of the websites below. Click on *create a blog.* Use your information from **A** to start a blog in English.

www.blogger.com   www.wordpress.com   _____

C After you create your blog, follow the steps below.

1 In your blog, write in English about your favorite computer or video game.
2 Give your writing a title.
3 When you finish writing, click *publish* or *post.*
4 Write a short email to your friends to tell them about your post.

What do you think?

1 Do you use your computer a lot? How often?
2 Today, there are many popular websites for meeting people (for friendship or love). Is meeting people online a good idea? Why?

Study and Education

Getting Ready

Look at the pictures. Then discuss these questions with a partner.

1 In your opinion, what is the best way to learn? Why?

☐ in a classroom ☐ at home ☐ online ☐ _____

2 There are many places to study and learn. Check (✓) the places you go to now.

☐ high school   ☐ music academy

☐ university   ☐ sports camp

☐ a language institute   ☐ test prep center

☐ art school   ☐ _____

3 Look at your answers to **2**. How are the places different? How are they the same?

CHAPTER 1 Doing Something Different

Before You Read
School Days

A Think about answers to these questions.

   1 Look at the photos of the people on the next page. What do you think they are studying?

   2 How many different places have you studied at? At which place have you learned the most?

B Discuss your answers with a partner.

Reading Skill
Recognizing Purpose

> Before you read, ask yourself: What am I reading? (*a newspaper article, an advertisement*) Also ask yourself: Why am I reading this text? (*for information, for fun*) These questions can help you be a better reader.

A Match the types of text with their purposes.

Type of Text		Purpose: You read this text to . . .
1 a newspaper article	_d_	**a** learn about something to buy.
2 a travel magazine	____	**b** learn about places to go on vacation.
3 a textbook	____	**c** get information about things happening in your school.
4 a student newsletter	____	**d** learn about things happening in your city or the world.
5 an advertisement	____	**e** learn new information about a school subject (e.g. math, science).

B Look quickly at the website on the next page. Then answer the questions below.

   1 What is the purpose of this passage?

      _____

   2 What can you learn from this passage?
      In this passage, I can learn about _____

      _____ .

C Read the website on the next page. Think about your purpose for reading it. Then answer the questions on page 24.

Setting high standards. As you begin this unit, set a goal with your classmates for reading fluency. Setting a goal together and then helping each other reach that goal can help you be a better reader.

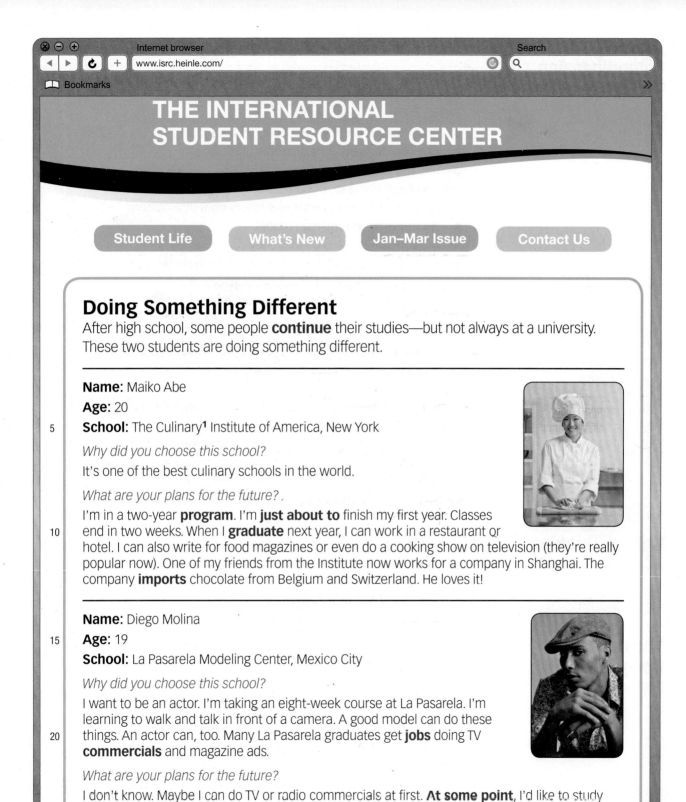

THE INTERNATIONAL STUDENT RESOURCE CENTER

Student Life   **What's New**   **Jan–Mar Issue**   **Contact Us**

Doing Something Different

After high school, some people **continue** their studies—but not always at a university. These two students are doing something different.

Name: Maiko Abe

Age: 20

5 **School:** The Culinary[1] Institute of America, New York

Why did you choose this school?

It's one of the best culinary schools in the world.

What are your plans for the future?

I'm in a two-year **program**. I'm **just about to** finish my first year. Classes
10 end in two weeks. When I **graduate** next year, I can work in a restaurant or
hotel. I can also write for food magazines or even do a cooking show on television (they're really
popular now). One of my friends from the Institute now works for a company in Shanghai. The
company **imports** chocolate from Belgium and Switzerland. He loves it!

Name: Diego Molina

15 **Age:** 19

School: La Pasarela Modeling Center, Mexico City

Why did you choose this school?

I want to be an actor. I'm taking an eight-week course at La Pasarela. I'm
learning to walk and talk in front of a camera. A good model can do these
20 things. An actor can, too. Many La Pasarela graduates get **jobs** doing TV
commercials and magazine ads.

What are your plans for the future?

I don't know. Maybe I can do TV or radio commercials at first. **At some point**, I'd like to study
acting here in Mexico or in Los Angeles.

---

[1] If something is **culinary** it is related to food and cooking.

Reading Comprehension
Check Your Understanding

A **Choose the correct answers.**

1 Which kind of school is NOT talked about in the passage?
   a cooking   **b** business   **c** modeling

2 Which sentence about Maiko is true?
   a She works in Europe right now.
   b She can do many jobs after she graduates.
   c She plans to study in Shanghai.

3 Why is Diego going to modeling school?
   a He wants to learn to walk and talk in front of a camera.
   b He wants to be a fashion model.
   c He wants to make a lot of money.

4 What is the meaning of the title *Doing Something Different?*
   a At university, there are many different classes.
   b Doing something different in school makes you a better student.
   c After high school, some people keep studying, but not at a university.

B **Read each sentence. Who is it about? Check (✔) Maiko or Diego. In some cases, both names are possible.**

		Maiko	Diego
1	This person is studying in the United States now.		
2	This person might study in the United States in the future.		
3	This person can work in television after graduating.		
4	This person has one more year to study.		

Critical Thinking

C 1 What can Maiko and Diego do when they finish school? Write the ideas from the passage. Then add one more idea for each person.
   2 Whose school is more interesting to you: Maiko's or Diego's? Why?

Vocabulary Comprehension
Definitions

A **Match each word with its definition. The words in blue are from the passage.**

1 continue _____ *C*
2 program _____
3 graduate _____
4 import _____
5 job _____
6 just about to _____
7 commercial _____
8 at some point _____

a somewhere in the future
b going to very soon
c to keep doing something
d the work you do for money
e a course of study in a school
f an advertisement on the radio or on TV
g to finish school or university
h to bring something into a country from another country

B Answer the questions below. Discuss your answers with a partner.

1 Do you want to continue studying English? For how long?

_____

2 Are you a high school graduate? If you are, when did you graduate? If not, when will you graduate?

_____

3 What kind of job do you want to have in the future?

_____

4 What is your favorite TV commercial?

_____

A There are five different contractions in the passage on page 23. Write each contraction below. Then write the two words that make up the contraction.

passage on page 23

Vocabulary Skill
Contractions

> In spoken English and informal writing, it is common to use contractions. For example, *I'm* is a contraction of *I* and *am*. The apostrophe (') shows that letters are missing in the word.

	Contraction	Two words
1	It's	It is
2	_____	_____
3	_____	_____
4	_____	_____
5	_____	_____

B Read the sentences. Do you know the contractions for the words in blue? Write them on the line.

1 Tim (is not) in school today. (He is) sick.   isn't / He's
2 Mary Ann does not speak Spanish.   _____
3 Who is that man? What is his name?   _____
4 There is a movie on TV now.   _____
5 That is Paul. He is an actor.   _____

C Complete the interview below. Use the contractions from **A** and **B** above.

> **An interview with Kira Foley from The Martial Arts Institute**
> **Interviewer:** What class are you taking?
> **Kira:** (1) _____ taking a taekwondo class twice a week.
> **Interviewer:** (2) _____ taekwondo?
> **Kira:** (3) _____ a Korean martial art. (4) _____ taking the class for fun and exercise.
> **Interviewer:** Is this your first time studying taekwondo?
> **Kira:** No, it (5) _____. I took a class last summer.
> **Interviewer:** (6) _____ your instructor?
> **Kira:** His name is Kim Hae Chul. (7) _____ a good teacher.
> **Interviewer:** Does he speak Korean in class?
> **Kira:** No, he (8) _____. He speaks English.

Before You Read
Weekend Classes

A **Think about answers to these questions.**

1 In your country, do students go to extra classes in the evening or on the weekend? What classes do they take?
2 Some people take classes for fun. Do you? What do you study?

B **Discuss your answers with a partner.**

Reading Skill
Skimming

You *skim* to get a general idea about a text. Don't read every word. Look only at photos, titles, words in bold, and important words.

A **On the next page, there is information about four workshops. Skim this information. What is each workshop about? Match each workshop to its description.**

1 Workshop 1 is about _____.   **a** travel
2 Workshop 2 is about _____.   **b** acting
3 Workshop 3 is about _____.   **c** test preparation
4 Workshop 4 is about _____.   **d** meeting people

B **Read the advertisement on the next page. Were your answers in A correct?**

C **Read the advertisement again. Then answer the questions on page 28.**

Learning to read in English is a valuable skill to develop. Good readers do well in all areas of learning. When you read well you have something meaningful to talk about, and you also have something meaningful to write about. Take the chance today to talk to someone or write something about what you are learning in your English class.

The Learning Center, Toronto

We have evening and weekend workshops[1] on . . .

test preparation — meeting people and making friends — jobs and making money

travel and language learning

Some of this month's workshops:

5 **① Get good grades!**

Do you forget information and do **poorly** on tests?
In this workshop, you can learn how to . . .

- remember more (95 percent of what you read).
- think quickly and read **fast** (400 words per minute!).
10 - do well on tests and get high **scores**.

② Find true love . . . today!

Are you single and **shy**? Is it hard for you to talk to people?
In this workshop, you can learn how to . . .

- talk to people: start a **conversation** with anyone.
15 - be more friendly and **outgoing**.
- understand a person's body language.

③ You're on TV!

Many actors get their start in television and radio commercials.
You can too!
20 In this workshop, you can learn how to . . .

- act in TV ads.
- use your voice on the radio.
- get TV or radio jobs.

④ See the world . . . for free!

25 Traveling is **expensive**. But you can see the world for very little money!
In this workshop, you can learn how to . . .

- get **discounts** (50–80 percent) on plane tickets.
- travel with your friends for free.
- see the world by cruise ship . . . for $1 per day!
30 You can also take this course online at **http://tlc.heinle.com**.

[1] A **workshop** is a one- or two-day practical class about a topic.

Reading Comprehension
Check Your Understanding

A **Choose the correct answers.**

1 Workshop 1 does NOT teach students _____.
   a how to read faster   **b** how to think faster   **c** how to write better

2 After you take Workshop 2, you will be able to _____.
   a talk to people more easily   **b** get married   **c** find someone who is shy

3 If you want to _____, take Workshop 3.
   a be a school teacher   **b** travel around the world   **c** act in TV and radio ads

4 At the end of Workshop 4, you will be able to _____.
   a work for an airline   **b** travel for little or no money   **c** always travel for free

B **Read the statements below. Check (✔) the workshop that each statement describes.**

		Workshop			
		1	2	3	4
a	You can learn how to make friends in this workshop.				
b	In this workshop, you'll learn how to plan your summer vacation.				
c	Want to understand difficult test questions? Take this workshop!				
d	If you take this workshop, you'll learn how to look good on camera.				

Critical Thinking

C **1** Which workshop is most interesting to you? Why?
   2 Which workshop can you do online? Think about the other three workshops. Would they be easy to do online?

Vocabulary Comprehension
Words in Context

A **In each sentence, (circle) the best answer. The words in blue are from the passage.**

1 A (turtle / horse) runs fast.

2 A cell phone is $100. You get a ten percent discount, so you pay ($90 / $110).

3 Liam does poorly in school because he (always / never) studies.

4 My new laptop was very expensive. It cost (very little / a lot of money).

5 Diana is so (shy / outgoing)! She hates talking to new people.

6 In my conversation class, we (speak / write) English.

7 Bill and Karen are watching a soccer game on TV. Bill asks, "What's the score?" Mary answers, "(It's 4 to 2 / It's at 7:30)."

B Answer the questions below. Discuss your answers with a partner.

1 Do you usually do poorly on tests or get high scores?

_____

2 Are you a shy or an outgoing person?

_____

3 What is the most expensive store you know?

_____

4 Which do you like more: a good movie or a good conversation?

_____

A Read the sentences.

> *Slow* and *quick* are adjectives. Add *-ly* to make an adverb.

Bill is a **slow** eater.
(adj.)

Bill eats **slowly**.
(adv.)

Jane is a **quick** thinker.
(adj.)

Jane thinks **quickly**.
(adv.)

> Look at the change in spelling.

The girl is **happy**. She's smiling.
(adj.)

The girl is smiling **happily**.
(adv.)

Vocabulary Skill
-ly Adverbs

> In the passage, you saw the words *quickly* and *poorly*. These are adverbs. They tell us how something is done. Many adverbs end in *-ly*.

B Complete the chart with the adverbs. Pay attention to the spelling.

Adjective	Adverb	Adjective	Adverb
quiet		busy	
loud		soft	
angry		nervous	
easy		neat	

C In each sentence, (circle) the correct word.

1 Eva is speaking (loud / loudly). Everyone can hear her.
2 Please be (quiet / quietly)! You're in a library.
3 You can talk, but please speak (soft / softly).
4 Don't eat so (quick / quickly)!
5 I am so (nervous / nervously)! There's a big exam tomorrow.
6 I always do (poor / poorly) on tests.

Real Life Skill
Completing a School
Application Form

A school application
asks about you and
your education.

A Read about one person's education below. Answer the questions.

School	City/Country	Dates (to/from)	Diploma/Degree
Universidad Complutense de Madrid	Madrid, Spain	2005–2009	Major: Mathematics
Colegio Parque Conde de Orgaz	Madrid, Spain	2001–2005	High school diploma

1 Is the person a university graduate? What was his major?

2 What other subjects can you study at university? Discuss with a partner.

B Look at the application form. Complete it with your information.

The Global Language School   Application Form

1 Name _____
           Last Name(s)   First Name   Middle Name(s)

2 Mailing Address _____
                          Street Address

_____
           City   State (or Province)   Postal Code   Country

3 Telephone Number
       (_____) _____
   Telephone number with country / area code

4 Email Address _____

5 Date of Birth _____ / _____ / _____
                          Year   Month   Day

6 Your Education:

School	City/Country	Dates (to/from)	Diploma/Degree

7 English Level: ☐ beginner   ☐ intermediate   ☐ advanced

   IELTS/TOEIC/TOEFL® score (if known): _____

What do you think?

What are your plans for the future? Would you like to *do something different*? If so, what would you do?

Work Choices

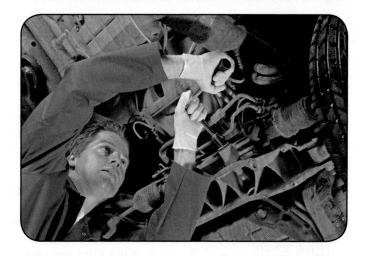

Getting Ready

Discuss these questions with a partner.

flight attendant	lawyer	journalist
programmer	sales clerk	mechanic
secretary/receptionist	taxi driver	waiter/waitress

1 Look at the job names in the box. Which jobs are in the pictures above?
2 Can you think of three more jobs?
3 Do you have a job? Is your job full-time or part-time?
   If you don't have a job, what do you want to be in the future?

CHAPTER 1 One Man, 52 Jobs

Before You Read
On the Job

A **Think about answers to these questions.**

1 Is it important to get a job quickly after graduating? Why?

2 Look at the words in the box. How are the words related?

> work   job   occupation   university   future

3 Look at the photo on the next page. What do you think this man's job is?

B **Discuss your answers with a partner.**

Reading Skill
Scanning

> You *scan* to find information fast. When you scan, you move your eyes quickly. You don't read every word; you only look for the information you need.

A **Look at the passage on the next page. Read only the title and the first paragraph. Then answer the question below.**

What is the passage about?
a a person with many jobs
b a good job for students
c a man who started his own company

B **Scan the passage on the next page. Find answers to the questions below.**

1 What was Sean Aiken's problem after college?

_____

2 What was Aiken's goal?

_____

3 How long did Aiken work at each job?

_____

4 What was Aiken's favorite job?

_____

5 What does Aiken do today?

_____

C **Now read the entire passage. Check your answers in B. Then answer the questions on page 34.**

> **Reading gives you something interesting to talk about!** When you read something interesting, don't just keep it to yourself. Share what you are reading with others. Even if you disagree with what you have read, you have something interesting to talk about.

dairy cows being milked

One Man, 52 Jobs

After graduating from college, Sean Aiken knew he would need to find a job soon. The problem was that he wasn't sure what kind of work he wanted to do.

One night at the dinner table, his father **encouraged** him to do what he liked most. His
5 father said he had worked his whole life doing a job he didn't really **enjoy**. Aiken wanted a different future. That night, he **promised** himself that he would find something that he was passionate[1] about.

Aiken **set a goal** to work a new job each week for a year. That's 52 **occupations** in one year. And he did it! One week, as a dairy farmer, he milked cows every morning. Then, in
10 another week, he was an astronomer studying the night sky. Aiken's favorite job, though, was teaching. He learned he was happiest when he was helping others.

Aiken also learned that it's OK to not know what you want to do **right away**. He wrote a book about his **experiences**, and today he tells his story to college and university students. His message? *You'll find your perfect job one day.* **After all**, Aiken found his.

---

[1] If you are **passionate** about something, you have strong feelings about it.

Reading Comprehension
Check Your Understanding

A Choose the correct answers.

1 What did Sean Aiken want to do after graduating from college?
   a He wanted to be a teacher.
   b He didn't know what to do.
   c He wanted to travel to Europe.

2 What did Aiken's father encourage him to do?
   a get a job he enjoyed doing
   b work one job his whole life
   c work for his father for one year

3 Which of these jobs is NOT talked about in the passage?
   a astronomer
   b dairy farmer
   c pilot

4 What did Aiken learn by working so many different jobs?
   a that working is very difficult and not fun
   b that it is okay to take your time finding a job
   c that people should get a job right after college

B Read the sentences below. Check (✔) true (T) or false (F). If the statement is false, change it to make it true.

		T	F
1	Aiken's father wanted him to do something he was passionate about.		
2	Aiken wanted to do what his father did.		
3	Aiken tried being a teacher.		
4	Today, Sean gives students advice about finding the perfect job.		

Critical Thinking

C 1 Do you think one week is long enough to know if a job is good or not?
   2 In your opinion, is Sean Aiken's life interesting? Why or why not?

Vocabulary Comprehension
Odd Word Out

A For each group of words, (circle) the word that does not belong. The words in blue are from the passage.

1	hobby	occupation	job
2	encouraged	supported	disagreed
3	later	right away	next time
4	promised	lied	guaranteed
5	make a plan	set a goal	take a chance
6	after all	in the end	from the start
7	enjoyed	hated	disliked
8	try something	experience	stay home

B Complete the sentences. Use a word in blue from **A**.

1 Don't keep this a secret! Tell everyone the news _____.
2 I quit my job because I want to try a new _____.
3 I have _____ to get a job this summer.
4 I really _____ playing soccer with my friends on the weekend.

A Read the email message below. Underline the words that mean *work*.

Vocabulary Skill
Synonyms for *Work*

In the passage *One Man, 52 Jobs*, you saw the words *job* and *occupation*. In English, there are many words that mean the same as *work*.

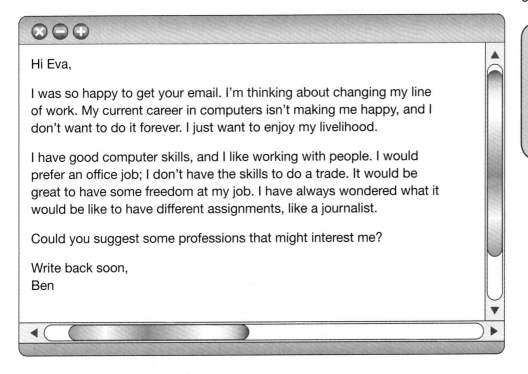

Hi Eva,

I was so happy to get your email. I'm thinking about changing my line of work. My current career in computers isn't making me happy, and I don't want to do it forever. I just want to enjoy my livelihood.

I have good computer skills, and I like working with people. I would prefer an office job; I don't have the skills to do a trade. It would be great to have some freedom at my job. I have always wondered what it would be like to have different assignments, like a journalist.

Could you suggest some professions that might interest me?

Write back soon,
Ben

B Complete each sentence with an underlined word from **A**. You might have to change the form of the word.

1 My first _____ for the newspaper was a story about the mayor!
2 Being a doctor or a teacher is a(n) _____, being a carpenter or a mechanic is a(n) _____.
3 In the past, most people had one job their whole life. But today, many people change their _____ often.
4 In my _____ as a baker, I must start work early in the morning.

CHAPTER 2 Working Holiday

Before You Read
On Holiday

A **Think about answers to these questions.**

1 What do people usually do on holiday? Check (✔) your answers.

☐ go to the beach   ☐ rest   ☐ study or work a lot
☐ wake up early   ☐ travel   ☐ _____

2 Look at the title of the passage on the next page. Look at the photos. What do you think a *working holiday* is?

B **Discuss your answers with a partner.**

Reading Skill
Understanding Main Ideas

> Headings are often at the start of a paragraph or part of a passage. Headings usually tell us the main idea of a paragraph or section of a passage. The main idea is the most important idea in a passage.

A **Read the headings below.**

Getting Started

Things to Bring with You

Types of Travel Projects

~~What Is a Working Holiday?~~

How Long Can I Work in Another Country?

B Read the information in the brochure on the next page. What is the main idea of each section (1–5)? Write the correct heading from **A** in the passage.

C Read the whole passage again. Then answer the questions on page 38.

> **Being a good reader requires mental attention.** Learning to be a good reader requires work. Don't be discouraged if at first it is hard. Keep practicing and you'll get better!

WORKING Holiday

① *What is a Working Holiday?*

A working holiday is a great way to see the world *and* **earn** money at the same time. Every year, thousands of students travel and work in other countries. Some do it because they want to learn a **skill** (for example, how to speak a
5 second language). Others just want to have fun. Often, you can do both!

② Today, there are many companies that can help you get started. Usually these companies can help you get a job and plan your **trip**. You usually pay for your own travel **expenses** (for example, your airfare and taxi fares).

③ What kind of work and travel **projects** can
10 you do? Here are some ideas!
You can . . .

- work for a popular teen magazine in the United Kingdom.
- teach music or sports to children in
15 Madagascar.
- work on a Norwegian cruise ship or at an Argentinean ski resort.
- work at an amusement park (for example, Disneyland) in the United States.

④ 20 Some people go for a month. Some others stay for six months to a year. What do you what to do? Think about your goals and then decide.

⑤ Here are some **tips** from other students about what to bring on your trip:
- Bring an ATM card. You might need **cash** for food, clothes, or travel.
- Make two or three copies of important **documents** (for example, your
25 passport).

Have fun!

Reading Comprehension

Check Your Understanding

A Choose the correct answers.

1 What is the meaning of the title *Working Holiday*?
  a Many people don't take holidays because they have to work.
  b In some jobs, people get a lot of holidays.
  c You can get a job and take a vacation at the same time.

2 According to the passage, why do people take working holidays?
  a to have fun and see the world
  b to find a place to live
  c to visit their relatives in other countries

3 How long can you work in another country?
  a It is different for everyone.
  b You can work for six months or a year.
  c You can only work for one month.

4 What does the passage say about money?
  a Your boss will pay for your travel expenses.
  b You should have an ATM card to get money.
  c You need a lot of money to take a working holiday.

B The passage has a few ideas for jobs to do while on working holidays. Match the jobs with the place mentioned in the passage.

You can . . .		in . . .
1 work on a cruise ship	_____	a the United States
2 teach sports or music	_____	b Argentina
3 work for a magazine	_____	c Norway
4 work at a ski resort	_____	d Madagascar
5 work at an amusement park	_____	e the United Kingdom

Critical Thinking

C 1 Which travel project is interesting to you? Why?
2 The passage has two travel tips. Are they good tips? Add one more tip.

Vocabulary Comprehension

Definitions

A Match each word with its definition. The words in blue are from the passage.

1 cash	_____	a	to get money or other things by working
2 document	_____	b	paper money or coins
3 earn	_____	c	an ability to do something
4 expenses	_____	d	a period of travel, usually for a short time
5 project	_____	e	a plan or a piece of work you do
6 skill	_____	f	a helpful idea
7 tip	_____	g	things you spend money on
8 trip	_____	h	a piece of paper, usually with important information on it

B Answer the questions below. Discuss your answers with a partner.

1 Name a skill you have.

_____

2 How do you earn money to spend on holiday?

_____

3 On your last trip, where did you go?

_____

4 Write one travel tip for people visiting your city.

_____

A Match a word from the box with a word below to make a compound noun.

back	boy	credit	guide	home
lap	sun	suit	travel	

1 _____ case   2 _____ book   3 _____ top

4 _____ glasses   5 _____ pack   6 _____ work

7 _____ friend   8 _____ agent   9 _____ card

B Which compound nouns in A are one word? Which are two words? Discuss with a partner. You can use your dictionary to help you.

C Imagine that this summer you plan to work in Greece for two months. Which items from A do you want to take with you? Circle them.

Vocabulary Skill
Compound Nouns

A compound noun joins two words to make one word (for example, *air* + *fare* = *airfare*). Sometimes, two words are used to talk about one thing (for example, *debit card*).

Real Life Skill
Reading a Job Ad

Job ads (sometimes called *want ads*) usually tell you about the hours, the pay, and the skills needed to do the job. In many job ads, single words or short sentences are used.

A Read the ad below.

——— DJ Needed! ———

DJ2Day is a small company. We need three new DJs to work with us NOW. This is a great part-time job for a student.

Job: about 10–15 hours a week at different locations: company parties, weddings, nightclubs

Looking for: an outgoing, fun, lively person. Knows all kinds of music. 18 and over only.

Pay: $30 an hour

Contact: Email us with information about yourself at jobs@dj2day.heinle.com.

B Look at the ad in A. Answer the questions.

1 What is the job in the ad? _____
2 What is the name of the company? _____
3 When does the job start? _____
4 How often do you work? _____
5 Where do you work? _____
6 What is the pay? _____
7 What skills do you need? _____
8 How can you contact the company? _____

C With a partner, make your own job ad. Use the example in A to help you.

D Exchange your ad with another pair. Answer the questions in B about their ad.

What do you think?

1 If you could have any job in the world for two weeks, what would you want to do? Why?
2 What is more important to you: money or happiness? Why?

PRO stands for **P**review, **R**ead, **O**rganize. This reading strategy will help you build your reading fluency by helping you to organize and understand what you read.

Preview

Preview means to look at the passage before you read. When you preview the passage, follow these three easy steps:

1 Read the title on the next page. What do you think you will learn from the passage?
2 Look at the pictures for the passage. What do they show? From the title and pictures, what do you think the passage is about?

3 Look for any words in the passage that are in *italics*. These will be important words in the passage. What words in the passage on the next page are in *italics*?

Read

Now, *read Can the Internet be bad for you?* When you read, check your answers from the *preview* stage.

Organize

The final step of **PRO** is to *organize* the information to help you remember what you have read. One way is by creating a word web. A word web can help you easily see how the information in the passage is organized.

A **Here is an incomplete word web based on the passage *Can the Internet be bad for you?* on the next page. Complete the rest of the word web using the information in the passage.**

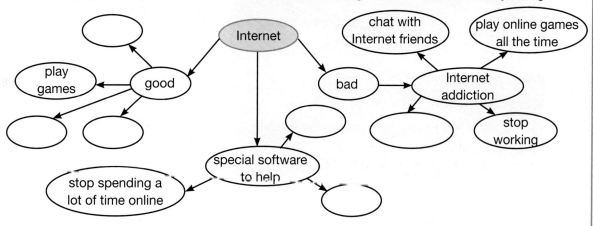

B **Look at the word web closely. Would you organize the ideas of the passage differently? Discuss the word web with a partner.**

Can the Internet be bad for you?

Spending your free time on the Internet can be fun. You can chat, share photos with friends, and play online games. But some people are
5 addicted to the Internet. They just can't turn it off.

Being online for many hours at a time does not mean you have a problem. The Internet is very useful.
10 Online, you can pay your bills, buy clothes, and read the news. There are many good reasons to spend time online.

However, people with an *Internet addiction* are online too much. They don't spend time with their friends and family. Instead, they spend their time chatting with their
15 Internet friends, people they have never met in real life. Some also play online games all day or night. Some people with Internet addictions even leave their jobs so they can spend even more time online!

People with Internet addictions don't just go online to shop, have fun, or do work. People who have this problem often go online because they want to escape the stress and
20 problems in their lives. Many internet addicts stop caring about their real lives, and focus only on their online lives.

One way Internet addicts can get help is by using special software. This software controls how much time someone can spend online. It tells the computer to turn off the internet after a certain amount of time. This helps people focus on real life. The software's goal is to teach people to use the Internet for good reasons and not just as an escape.

247 words   **Time taken** _____

Reading Comprehension

Choose the correct answers. Use the word web in A to help you.

1 What is the main idea of the article?
   a People should not spend time on the Internet.
   b The Internet is very good for people.
   c Spending too much time online is not good.
   d Families should use the Internet together.

2 Which is NOT a problem for people with Internet addiction?
   a They stop spending time with their family.
   b They might lose their jobs.
   c They learn to type very fast.
   d They stop caring about their real lives.

3 What does the article say about paying bills?
   a It should be done online.
   b It is a useful way to use the Internet.
   c People with Internet addiction do not pay their bills.
   d People save money when they pay bills online.

4 What way of helping people stop their Internet addiction does the passage talk about?
   a watching TV with friends
   b using special software
   c spending more hours at their office
   d getting a new job they really like

5 According to the passage, a person is most likely to become an Internet addict if _____ .
   a their life is stressful and has problems
   b their job is boring
   c they enjoy online gaming
   d they have a lot of online friends

SELF CHECK

Write a short answer to each of the following questions.

1. Have you ever used the PRO method before?

   ☐ Yes ☐ No ☐ I'm not sure.

2. Do you practice PRO in your reading outside of English class?

   ☐ Yes ☐ No ☐ I'm not sure.

3. Do you think PRO is helpful? Why?

   _____

   _____

4. Which of the six reading passages in units 1–3 did you enjoy most? Why?

   _____

   _____

5. Which of the six reading passages in units 1–3 was easiest? Which was most difficult? Why?

   Easiest: _____

   Most difficult: _____

   Why? _____

   _____

6. What have you read in English outside of class recently?

   _____

   _____

7. How will you try to improve your reading fluency from now on?

   _____

   _____

   _____

   _____

Review Reading 1: Lifelong Learning

Fluency Practice

Time yourself as you read through the passage. Try to read as fluently as you can. Record your time in the Reading Rate Chart on page 176. Then answer the questions on the next page.

www.ASR_lifelonglearning.heinle.com

Lifelong Learning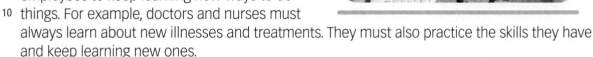

When you graduate from high school or university, is learning finished? The answer is *no*. In many countries, people continue learning all their lives. Why is lifelong learning important?

5 How can it help you?

Lifelong learning can be useful in many ways. People who want to change careers often return to study at a university. Some professions require employees to keep learning new ways to do

10 things. For example, doctors and nurses must always learn about new illnesses and treatments. They must also practice the skills they have and keep learning new ones.

Lifelong learning can help people stay healthy and independent. Many older people also feel that lifelong learning helps them stay close to young people. Lots of older people are now

15 learning how to use computers.

"I want to remain active . . . for my own health," said Mr. Salinas, a 91-year-old man taking computer classes. "I see my computer learning as . . . part of an active life and something that I can share . . . with my family."

175 words   Time taken _____

Reading Comprehension

Choose the correct answers.

1 What does *lifelong learning* mean?
   a You stop learning after high school.
   b You learn about life when you are a child.
   c You continue learning for your whole life.
   d You learn how to live for a very long time.

2 What does the article say about nurses?
   a They use the same information for many years.
   b They must learn new things all the time.
   c They did not use technology in the past.
   d They need to work independently.

3 Lifelong learning can help people _____.
   a be smarter than other people
   b live to be very old
   c stop being lazy
   d be healthy and independent

4 Which of the following might Mr. Salinas say?
   a "Going to computer class makes me feel tired."
   b "I don't like going to computer class because I don't understand."
   c "Now, I can send emails to my grandchildren."
   d "Computers are for kids! I like books and newspapers."

5 This article was most likely written for _____.
   a school children
   b working adults
   c computer teachers
   d doctors

Review Reading 2: Earning Power

Fluency Practice

Time yourself as you read through the passage. Try to read as fluently as you can. Record your time in the Reading Rate Chart on page 176. Then answer the questions on the next page.

ASR Financial Times: Special Report   **Earning Power**

Earning Power

Everyone wants a job that pays well. Some people stop school early because they want to start earning cash right away. Others spend years and years studying in school in order to get a better job. Which is best? Actually, studies show that in most jobs, the higher your education, the higher your earning power.

5   For example, in the United States, high school graduates can make about $30,400 a year. The people who do not finish high school average only $23,400 a year. Just having a document that says you finished high school means an extra $7,000!

If you stay in school, you can make more money. A person who goes to college and gets a bachelor's degree can make an average of $52,200. With a master's degree, he or she can
10 make about $62,000. And studies show that if a person gets a PhD, he or she can make $89,000 or more a year.

Of course, people with different occupations have different salaries. The chart below shows some average salaries for different professions in the United States.

We can learn an important lesson from this information. If you want to work and make
15 more money, spend more time in school.

Average Salaries for Common Occupations

Sales Clerk	High School Teacher	Firefighter	Accountant	Dentist
$20,000	$44,000	$48,000	$69,000	$159,000

178 words   **Time taken** _____

Reading Comprehension

Choose the correct answers.

1   Why does the passage say people stop high school early?
    a   They do not have a lot of money.
    b   They do not like going to school.
    c   They do not want to work hard.
    d   They want to start making money.

2   According to the passage, how can a person earn more money?
    a   by stopping high school
    b   by staying in school for a long time
    c   by working a part-time job in high school
    d   by starting a small business

3   Which of these ideas is mentioned in the passage?
    a   Everyone should get a master's degree.
    b   Graduating high school is important.
    c   A person should do the same job their whole life.
    d   A person with a PhD will not earn a lot of money.

4   According to the chart, which job pays the most money?
    a   dentist
    b   high school teacher
    c   photographer
    d   accountant

5   Why was this passage written?
    a   to make school more fun
    b   to encourage people to stay in school
    c   to help people who score poorly on tests
    d   to teach people how to set goals

The World of Sports

Getting Ready

Discuss these questions with a partner.

1   Look at the photos above. What sports are the people playing? How are these sports alike? How are they different?
2   What other sports do you know? Think of five.
3   What is your favorite sport?

Before You Read
Play Ball!

A Think about answers to these questions.

1 How do you *hit* a ball? *Kick* a ball? *Throw* a ball? For each verb, do the action.

2 Look at the passage on the next page. Read the title and look at the photos. Do you know this sport? How do you think you play this game?

B Discuss your answers with a partner.

Reading Skill
Reading for Details

When we read for details, we read slowly. For example, when we read instructions, we read carefully so we do not miss anything important.

A There are five paragraphs in the passage on the next page. Read only the first sentence of each paragraph. Then answer the question below.

You want to know how to play sepak takraw. Which paragraph(s) should you read? (Circle) the number of the paragraph(s).

B Carefully read the paragraph(s) you circled in **A**. Then (circle) the correct words to complete the sentences.

Sepak Takraw Game Rules

1 Players use a (large / small) ball.
2 There are (two / three) players on each team.
3 Players can use their (heads / hands) to pass the ball over the net.
4 Your team scores a point when the other team (kicks / drops) the ball.
5 There are (two / three) sets in a game.
6 To win a set, you must score (15 / 20) points.
7 To win the game, you must win (two / three) sets.

C Now read the entire passage on the next page. Then answer the questions on page 52.

Humor and reading. What is the funniest thing you have read in the past week? Reading comic strips can be a fun thing to do. Humor is often based on cultural issues. Reading and understanding humor in English can be a good way to learn more about the world.

1 Sports like soccer, baseball, and basketball are popular all over the world. Many countries also have their own national sports. These **traditional** games are often hundreds—or even thousands—of years old. Here is one example.

Sepak Takraw

2
5 Malaysia's national sport is sepak takraw (*sepak* means *kick*, and *takraw* means *woven*[1] *ball*). This fast-moving game is like both soccer and volleyball.

3
In sepak takraw, players move the ball like
10 they do in soccer and volleyball. Two **teams** (of three players each) **compete** by hitting a small ball across a net (like they do in volleyball). Players can use their heads, feet, shoulders, or knees to pass the ball to
15 the other team. But like in soccer games, players cannot use their hands.

4
Playing sepak takraw is a little like playing tennis, too. Like a tennis match, there are three sets[2] in a game. If one team drops the
20 ball, the other team gets a **point**. The first team to get 15 points **wins** a set. The winner of two sets wins the whole game.

5
The sport of sepak takraw is more than 1,000 years old. **Originally**, the native Malays played it. Later, the sport **spread** to other countries in Asia, including Thailand, Indonesia, and the
25 Philippines. Today, it is one of the most popular sports played in the Asian Games. There are also sepak takraw **clubs** in North America and Europe.

---

[1] Something that is **woven** is made like a basket with fibers crossing over and under each other.
[2] A **set** is a part of a game.

Reading Comprehension
Check Your Understanding

A **Choose the correct answers.**

1 Sepak takraw is played very _____.
   a slowly   **b** quickly   **c** rarely

2 The people of _____ first played sepak takraw.
   a Thailand   **b** the Philippines   **c** Malaysia

3 How is sepak takraw like volleyball?
   a Players cannot use their hands.
   b Players hit a ball across a net.
   c The game is divided into three parts.

4 How is sepak takraw like soccer?
   a Players cannot use their hands.
   b There are three sets in a game.
   c Players can only use their feet to hit the ball.

B **Read the sentences below. Check (✓) if the sentence is a main idea (M) or a detail (D) of the passage.**

		M	D
1	Sepak takraw is the national sport of Malaysia.		
2	The game is played with a small ball.		
3	When passing the ball, a player can use his head.		
4	Sepak takraw is played in many countries.		

Critical Thinking

C 1 Do you think sepak takraw is a fun game? Why or why not?
       2 Does your country have a national sport?

Vocabulary Comprehension
Words in Context

A **In each sentence, (circle) the best answer. The words in blue are from the passage.**

1 Kimonos are a kind of (traditional / modern) Japanese costume.
2 (Golf / Soccer) is always a team sport. You can't play it on your own.
3 Nick and Mario are always competing. They (often / never) work together.
4 In a spelling test, you get a point when you spell a word (correctly / wrong).
5 The player with the most points usually (loses / wins) the game.
6 Ricardo lives in Mexico, but he's originally from Brazil. He was born in (Mexico / Brazil).
7 If a fire spreads, it gets (larger / smaller)
8 The chess club has (one member / ten members). They play chess every day.

B Answer the questions below. Discuss your answers with a partner.

1 What is your favorite sports team?

_____

2 Think of a game you know. How do you get points to win the game?

_____

3 Does your school have any sports teams or clubs? Do they ever compete against other schools?

_____

4 What country is your favorite sport originally from?

_____

A Complete the word web below with words from the box.

baseball	basketball	compete	golf
hockey	kick	lose	rowing
score (a point)	sepak takraw	skiing	surfing
swimming	tennis	throw	win

Vocabulary Skill
Word Webs

When you link related words and ideas together, it is easier to remember them. A word web can help you organize and remember new vocabulary.

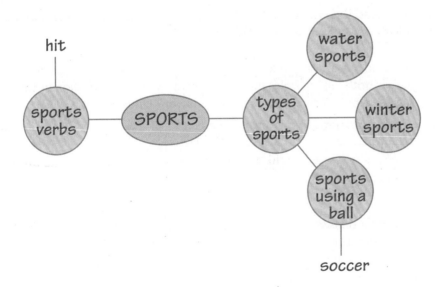

B Work with a partner. Add other words to the word web.

Before You Read
Sports Fans

A Think about answers to these questions.

1 Read the sentence below. What is a *sports fan*?

> Ian is a **fan** of the soccer team Manchester United. He knows all the players and watches all the games.

2 Are you a sports fan? Why or why not?

B Discuss your answers with a partner.

Reading Skill
Making Inferences

> When we read, the author does not tell us everything. We can guess some things because of the information in the passage. These guesses are called *inferences*.

A Read the title and the first two paragraphs of the passage on the next page. Then answer the question below.

What is this reading about?
a people's favorite sports
b why sports are important
c the money players make

B Now read the whole passage. As you read, think about this: What does each person think about sports?

C Does each person think sports bring people together (T), divide them (D), or both (B)? Circle the best answer. What information in the passage helped you choose your answer? Underline it.

Vlad	T	D	B
Kelly	T	D	B
Oba	T	D	B

D Read the passage on the next page again. Then answer the questions on page 56.

> **Group cohesiveness.** In language classes, students often sit in the same seat for every class, next to people they already know. In class today, move to a new seat and sit next to someone you do not know very well. Strengthening the cohesiveness of your class group will help all of you learn to read in English.

**UR WORLD**

HOME | NEWS | **SPORTS** | WEATHER | MEDIA | TRAVEL

Are sports important?

Sports are all around us. We watch and read sports news. There are
also sports bars and even sports-only channels on TV. In many
countries, **athletes** make millions of dollars every year. But why
are sports (like soccer and baseball) so important? They're only
5 games, right?

Our readers answer:

Vlad
(Kiev, Ukraine)

Sports bring people together. In 2006, our team qualified[1] for
the soccer World Cup for the first time. Everyone was happy.
Rich and poor, old and young, men and women—everyone
was dancing in the streets together!

**Kelly**
(Philadelphia, USA)

10 Sports bring people together, but **they divide them**, too. **Fans**
of different teams **fight** all the time—they yell and hit each
other. For example: My brother plays high school baseball. Last
week, his team played an important game. At the game, two
parents fought about a call.[2] Come on . . . baseball is only a
15 game! Sports are so **competitive** these days. It's all about
winning. When fights happen, the game isn't fun anymore.

Oba
(Abuja, Nigeria)

Right now, some of the world's best soccer players are from
African countries (Cameroon, Senegal, the Ivory Coast), and
the 2010 World Cup was in South Africa. Yes, some athletes
20 make a lot of money—maybe too much. But sporting **events**
(like the World Cup) bring **tourists** and money to countries
and help their people. And **that** was really good for Africa.

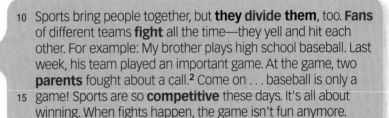

✉ Send us your opinion.

---

[1] If you **qualify** for something, you are good enough to compete.
[2] A **call** is a decision made in a sports game.

Reading Comprehension
Check Your Understanding

A **Choose the correct answers.**

1 What is the main idea of the passage?
  a Sports make people happy.
  b Players make a lot of money.
  c People have different opinions about sports.

2 Why are sports important for Oba?
  a They can bring tourists and money to a place.
  b The World Cup was in South Africa in 2010.
  c The best soccer players are African.

3 According to Kelly, when players and fans only think about winning, a game is not _____ .
  a important   **b** competitive   **c** fun

4 Why are sports important for Vlad?
  a His team was in the World Cup.
  b They bring people together.
  c Some players can get rich.

B **Read the sentences below. Find the words in the passage. Circle the correct answer.**

1 In line 10, **they** means (sports / people).
2 In line 10, **them** means (sports / people).
3 In line 22, **that** means (athletes / sporting events) bringing money to Africa.

Critical Thinking

C **1** In the passage, three people give their opinions. Who do you agree with? Why?
2 Think of one more reason sports are important or are not important. Tell your partner.

Vocabulary Comprehension
Words in Context

A **Read the sentences below. Check (✔) true (T) or false (F). If the statement is false, change it to make it true. The words in blue are from the passage.**

		T	F
1	An athlete is someone who watches sports on TV.		
2	If you divide something, you have two or more pieces.		
3	A fan of a sports team plays on the team.		
4	When two people fight, they are angry with each other.		
5	Your parents are your brother and sister.		
6	Hiking is a competitive sport.		
7	A lesson is a kind of event.		
8	A tourist visits another city or country on vacation.		

B Answer the questions below. Discuss your answers with a partner.

1. Name an important sports event. _____
2. Name a popular athlete. _____
3. Are you a competitive person? _____
4. Do you ever fight with your parents or friends? _____

A Read the paragraph below. Find the missing parts of speech for the word families in the chart below. Add the words to the chart.

Vocabulary Skill
Word Families

> In this chapter, you learned the word *competitive*. In Chapter 1, you learned the word *compete*. These words are in the same *word family*. You can build your vocabulary by learning word families.

Every year, my high school has a spelling competition. Students from different grades compete against each other for first prize: $5,000! This year, my friend Jon entered . . . and he won! At the end, the last two competitors were Jon and a girl named Angie. The winning word was sarcophagus. After Jon spelled it, everyone was quiet. Then the teacher said, "Congratulations. You're this year's winner!"

	Noun	Verb	Adjective
1	1. competition 2.		competitive
2	winner	win	winning

B Complete the sentences with the correct words from the chart in A.

1. Leo is so _____! He always wants to _____.
2. In the swimming race, one _____ was a boy named James.
3. Here's my lottery ticket. What are the _____ numbers?
4. There are five skaters in this year's ice-skating _____.

Real Life Skill
Dictionary Usage: Finding Past Tense Verbs

The base form of a verb (for example, *play*, *fight*) is always in a dictionary. The past tense of regular verbs (*played*) and irregular verbs (*fought*) is always given with the base form.

A Look at the dictionary entries for the verbs *lose* and *compete*. Answer the questions.

lose /luːz/ *v.* **lost** /lɒst/, **losing, loses**
to be defeated (in a competition or war): *Our team lost the basketball game.*

compete /kɒmˈpiːt/ *v.* **-peted, -peting, -petes**
to participate in a contest: *Our basketball team competed against another team and won.*

1 What is the simple past tense of *lose* and *compete*?
_____

2 Which verb is regular? _____

3 Which verb is irregular? _____

B Find the verbs below in your dictionary. Write the past tense form. Check (✔) if the verb is regular (R) or irregular (I).

	verb	past tense	R	I
1	bring			
2	divide			
3	drop			
4	get			
5	go			
6	hit			
7	kick			
8	make			
9	score			
10	throw			

What do you think?

1 There are many international sporting events (the World Cup, the Asian Games, the X Games, the Olympics). Which one would you most like to go to? Why?

2 There are many famous female athletes. Name three famous female athletes you know. What sports do they play?

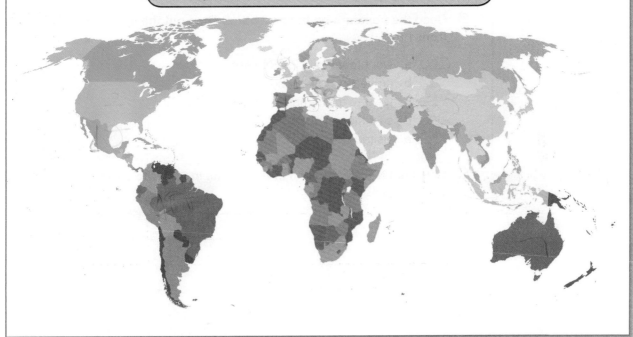

The World's Most Visited Countries*

1	France	6	The United Kingdom
2	The United States	7	Turkey
3	China	8	Germany
4	Spain	9	Malaysia
5	Italy	10	Mexico

*Source: the World Tourism Organization

Getting Ready

Discuss these questions with a partner.

1 Read the list of countries above. Can you find these places on the map?
2 In your opinion, why are these places popular?
3 Is there a city or country you want to visit? Why do you want to go there?

CHAPTER 1 A Postcard from Hong Kong

Before You Read
On the Road

A Think about answers to these questions.

1 Do you have any postcards? Where are they from?
2 Look at the postcard on the next page. Where is it from? What do you know about this city?

B Discuss your answers with a partner.

Reading Skill
Understanding the Order of Events

> Some passages tell us about an order of events. In these passages, you often see words about time, for example, *Monday, Tuesday, Wednesday, first, then, yesterday, today, tomorrow, morning, afternoon,* and *evening.*

A Look quickly at the postcard on the next page. Underline the time words you see (for example, days of the week, *then*, *yesterday*, *today*, and *tomorrow*).

B Read the postcard on the next page. Then put the events below in order from 1 to 5.

_____ **a** went to Victoria Peak to see the view
_1_ **b** arrived in Hong Kong
_____ **c** went to the Temple Street Night Market
_____ **d** saw the pandas
_____ **e** visited Disneyland

C When did Natalie do each of the events in **B**? Write a to e in the calendar below.

D Read the postcard again. Then answer the questions on page 62.

Scenic Hong Kong

Dear Jacquie,

Hello from Hong Kong! My class trip is almost over, and this city is the last stop[1] on our **tour**. We **arrived** here on Friday night, and I'm having a lot of fun.

5 On Saturday, we visited the top of Victoria Peak. The **view** of the city was **incredible**! I could see all of Hong Kong. There were also some nature trails[2] on the Peak. We went for a short walk, and then had **lunch** in the afternoon.

In the evening, I went with two friends to the Temple Street
10 Night Market. The streets were full of people selling food, clothes, jewelry, music, movies, electronics, and lots of other things. I bought some **souvenirs** to bring home. There were fortune tellers at the market, too. One told me, "You're going to fall in love soon." I hope she was right!

15 Yesterday, our group went to Disneyland. Yes, there's one here! We were there all day. The park was **crowded**, and the lines for rides were long. I waited an hour to go on Space Mountain (the roller coaster).
That was my favorite part of the trip!

20 Today is Monday. We're going to Ocean Park to see the pandas this afternoon.
We **return** home to Vancouver tomorrow.
See you soon!
Natalie

Jacquie Martin

22 Ridley Gardens

Vancouver, B.C.

Canada V6C 2C2

[1] The **last stop** on a trip is the last place you visit.
[2] A **trail** is a path, for example, through a forest.

Reading Comprehension
Check Your Understanding

A **Choose the correct answers.**

1 Natalie thinks Hong Kong is _____.
   a boring   **b** expensive   **c** enjoyable

2 Natalie visited Victoria Peak. What did she like the most?
   a the view of Hong Kong   **b** the nature trails   **c** the afternoon lunch

3 What did Natalie buy at the Temple Street Night Market?
   a food   **b** souvenirs   **c** jewelry

4 There were _____ people at Disneyland.
   a very few   **b** some   **c** a lot of

B **Read the sentences below. Check (✓) true (T) or false (F). If the statement is false, change it to make it true.**

		T	F
1	On her tour, Natalie visited Hong Kong first.		
2	Natalie's favorite ride at Disneyland was a roller coaster.		
3	Natalie lives in Canada.		

Critical Thinking

C 1 In your opinion, was Natalie's trip to Hong Kong fun? Why or why not?
   2 Which of the things Natalie did would you most like to do?

Vocabulary Comprehension
Words in Context

A **In each sentence, (circle) the best answer. The words in blue are from the passage.**

1 On his tour of France, Kentaro visited _____.
   a only one place   **b** many places

2 The exam is from 9:00 a.m. to noon. Please arrive at the school by
   _____.
   a 8:45 a.m.   **b** noon

3 You can get a good view of the city from _____.
   a the hotel workers   **b** the top of a tall building

4 The food at that restaurant is incredible. It is really very _____.
   a good   **b** bad

5 Lunch at school is from _____.
   a noon to 2:00 p.m.   **b** 7:00 to 9:00 p.m.

6 Which of these is a better souvenir?
   a a house   **b** a T-shirt

7 The bus was crowded this morning. There were _____ people.

    a very few   **b** a lot of

8 The party is from 7:00 to 11:00 p.m. I'll _____ home at 11:30 p.m.

    a leave   **b** return

B   **Answer the questions below. Discuss your answers with a partner.**

1 Do you have any souvenirs from your travels?

    _____

2 When do you usually arrive at school?

    _____

3 Where can you go to get a nice view of your city?

    _____

4 Which places in your city are the most crowded?

    _____

A   **Match each word with a definition.**

1	recall	_____	**a** to remember, to bring back to memory
2	reheat	_____	**b** to come back together
3	repay	_____	**c** to make something warm again
4	reunite	_____	**d** to look at something again carefully
5	reuse	_____	**e** to return money, to give back
6	review	_____	**f** to use something again

B   **Read these sentences and (circle) the correct word.**

1 I borrowed some money. I need to (repay / reuse) it next week.

2 Who is that woman? I can't (recall / review) her name.

3 This food is cold. Can you (review / reheat) it?

4 For the test tomorrow, please (reuse / review) pages 25–30 of your textbook.

5 This paper is still OK. You can (reuse / remake) it.

6 Last week, my father (reunited / reviewed) with his friends from school. They hadn't seen each other for 30 years!

Vocabulary Skill
The Prefix *re-*

In this chapter, you learned the word *return*. The prefix *re-* can come before a verb. It means *back* (for example, *re + turn =* to go back). *Re-* can also mean *again* (for example, *re + do =* to do something again).

Peer role models. Do you know someone who is a strong reader? What do they do that makes them a good reader? Think about what you can do to become more like the good readers you know.

CHAPTER 2 Destination: Singapore

Before You Read
Five-Star Hotels

A **Think about answers to these questions.**

1 What are the best hotels in your city?

2 What do you know about Singapore?

3 Do you know anything about the hotel in the passage?

B **Discuss your answers with a partner.**

Reading Skill
Scanning

> Remember: You *scan* to find information fast. You don't read every word. You only look for the information you need.

A **Scan the passage on the next page. Find answers to the questions below.**

1 What can you do for fun at the hotel? _____

_____

2 How long did it take to build the hotel? _____

_____

3 Who is Wolfgang Puck? _____

_____

4 How high are the buildings? _____

_____

5 How long is the pool? _____

_____

B **Read the information in the list. Then answer the question below, using your answers from A.**

For our trip, my family wants . . .
- a hotel in Singapore
- a view of the city
- a hotel where we can eat and swim
- a place to go shopping and find entertainment

Is the Marina Bay Sands Hotel a good place for your family to stay? Why?

_____

C **Now read the entire passage on the next page. Then answer the questions on page 66.**

Reasons for being a good reader. When learners are good readers they make progress in all areas of language learning. Becoming a good reader will help you accomplish your goals for using English.

 **UR WORLD** | HOME | NEWS | SPORTS | WEATHER | MEDIA | TRAVEL

Destination: Singapore
Place to stay: Marina Bay Sands Hotel
Rating: ★★★★★

The Marina Bay Sands Hotel in Singapore is more than just a hotel; it's like a small city. There's a museum, a luxury[1] shopping center, a casino, and two theaters. If that isn't
5 enough, it also has the most **impressive** view of Singapore.

Background[2]
Building a hotel as **huge** as the Marina Bay Sands was a challenge. The hardest part of the project was making the rooftop observation deck, called The Skypark. The deck stretches over all three of the hotel's 55-story towers, and it's as long as the Eiffel Tower
10 is **tall**. To build it, engineers had to use the same technology used to make some of the world's biggest bridges.[3] In all, more than 15,000 people worked night and day for almost three years to finish the project.

Dining
Many world-famous **chefs** have opened restaurants at the Marina Bay Sands, including
15 Mario Batali and Wolfgang Puck. **Guests** can **feast** on all kinds of delicious food, from steak to Singaporean street food like noodles or curry.

Activities
Learn something new at the hotel's Art & Science Museum, go ice-skating, or just **relax** at the pool. At
20 150 meters, it's the world's longest roof-top pool, so you can go swimming 200 meters up in the sky!

The Marina Bay Sands has so much to offer. There's something here for everyone!

[1] **Luxury** is very great comfort, especially surrounded by beautiful or expensive things.
[2] Someone or something's **background** is information about their or its past.
[3] A **bridge** is a thing that crosses over a river or road so people can go from one side to the other.

Reading Comprehension
Check Your Understanding

A Choose the correct answers.

1 Who most likely stays at the Marina Bay Sands Hotel?
   a university students and backpackers
   b poor families with many children
   c people who like luxury

2 What can guests do at the hotel?
   a They can go shopping.
   b They can play tennis.
   c They can take cooking classes.

3 The Skypark _____.
   a has a great view of Singapore
   b is 500 meters high
   c is a shopping center

4 What is NOT mentioned in the article?
   a the restaurants at the hotel
   b the price of a hotel room
   c how many people built the hotel

B Read the sentences below. Which section of the passage does each sentence belong in? Write a, b, or c. One sentence does not belong in the passage. Mark it with an X.

> **a** Background   **b** Dining   **c** Activities

1 _____ Famous singers and musicians often play concerts at the hotel.
2 _____ Many restaurants are open until 2:00 a.m.
3 _____ Every floor has a laundry room for guests to wash their clothes.
4 _____ The Marina Bay Sands is owned by a company from Las Vegas.

Critical Thinking

C 1 Do you think the Marina Bay Sands Hotel is a nice place to stay? Why or why not?
   2 What part of the hotel do you like the most?

A Read the sentences below. Check (✔) true (T) or false (F). If the statement is false, change it to make it true. The words in blue are from the passage.

		T	F
1	Vic is 130 centimeters tall, and Carl is 180. Vic is tall and Carl is short.		
2	When you are visiting your friend's house, you are the guest.		
3	The Eiffel Tower in Paris is a very impressive building.		
4	Pollution is a huge problem for the world. It can't be fixed in only a short time.		
5	In most houses, people sleep in the dining room.		
6	A chef is someone who reports the news.		
7	When you relax, you are more calm.		
8	A sandwich and some apples is a feast.		

B Complete the sentences below. Discuss your answers with a partner.

1 _____ is tall.
2 To relax, I usually _____.
3 When a guest visits your house, you should _____.
4 In my country, people have a feast to celebrate _____.

A Look at the adjectives in the table. Are they usually used to describe height, weight (or size), or both? Can they be used for people, things, or both? Check (✓) all the correct boxes for each adjective.

	tall	short	huge	massive	chubby	fat	tiny	slim	petite	giant
height										
size or weight										
people										
things										

B Choose six of the words in the table, and write true sentences.

1 _____.
2 _____.
3 _____.
4 _____.
5 _____.
6 _____.

> Tall and short, big and small, fat and thin. These are very simple adjectives used to describe height, size, and weight. You can show your understanding of English by using more descriptive adjectives.

Real Life Skill
Writing an Informal Note

We often write informal postcards, letters, or emails to friends or family members. There are certain words you can use to open and close these kinds of notes.

A Read the postcard. Then answer the questions below.

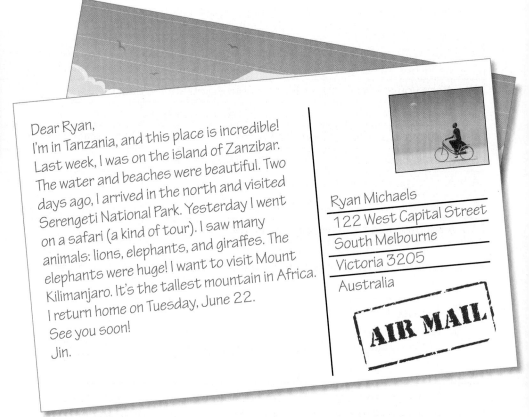

Dear Ryan,
I'm in Tanzania, and this place is incredible! Last week, I was on the island of Zanzibar. The water and beaches were beautiful. Two days ago, I arrived in the north and visited Serengeti National Park. Yesterday I went on a safari (a kind of tour). I saw many animals: lions, elephants, and giraffes. The elephants were huge! I want to visit Mount Kilimanjaro. It's the tallest mountain in Africa. I return home on Tuesday, June 22.
See you soon!
Jin.

Ryan Michaels
122 West Capital Street
South Melbourne
Victoria 3205
Australia

AIR MAIL

1 Jin starts the postcard to his friend with *Dear Ryan*. He ends it with *See you soon!* How else can you start and end a postcard to a friend? Check (✓) your answers.

Openings: ☐ Hi, ☐ Greetings! ☐ Dear Sir or Madam:
Closings: ☐ Yours sincerely, ☐ All the best! ☐ Take care,

2 Look at the address on the postcard. Do you write addresses differently in your country?

B Think of a city or country you want to visit. Imagine you are there on vacation. Write a postcard to a classmate or someone else you know. Tell them about your trip.

What do you think?

A *city guidebook* tells tourists about things to do and see in a city. Make a city guidebook for your city. Think about the questions below. Don't forget to give extra information about the places you choose.

1 What are two good restaurants in your city?
2 What are two places to stay (hotels, inns, youth hostels)?
3 What are three places to see or things to do? How do you get there?

Comparing Cultures

QUICK CULTURE QUIZ

(Circle) the correct answer for each sentence below.

1
In Argentina, male and female friends often (kiss / wave) when they meet.

2
In the United States, many children leave their parents' house at age (18 / 28). They often live with roommates.

3
Kerry lives in Korea. On her birthday, she asked some friends to have dinner at a restaurant. At the end, (Kerry paid for everyone / Kerry's friends paid for her).

4
In (England / Spain), people often eat dinner at 9:30 or 10:00 p.m.

5
Are you visiting a Brazilian friend's home for dinner? It's nice to bring a small gift. But don't give gifts or flowers in (red and green / black and purple). These colors are said to be bad luck.

Getting Ready

Discuss these questions with a partner.
1 Take the quiz above. Check your answers on the next page. Were your answers correct?
2 Are any of the customs in the quiz the same in your country?
3 How can you learn about the customs of another country?

Before You Read
Mind Your Manners

A **Think about answers to these questions.**

1 Do you ever eat food from other countries? Which countries?

2 Read the sentences below. What is another example of good and bad manners?

> "Don't eat so fast. It's bad manners."

> "It's good manners to chew with your mouth closed."

3 Look quickly at the passage on the next page. What examples of table manners do you think it will give?

B **Discuss your answers with a partner.**

Reading Skill
Identifying Similarities and Differences

> When we *compare* things, we look for ways they are the same (or similar) and the ways they are different. Looking at how a passage makes comparisons can increase your understanding of a passage.

A **The passage on the next page compares eating customs in two countries. Read the passage. How are the countries different? Complete the chart below.**

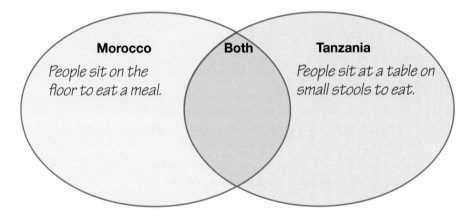

Morocco

People sit on the floor to eat a meal.

Both

Tanzania

People sit at a table on small stools to eat.

B **Read the passage again. How are the countries the same? Write two answers in the *Both* part of the chart in A. Then answer the questions on page 72.**

Reading helps you in the world. Being a good reader in both your first language and in English is useful to you and your community. You will benefit as a citizen of the world as you read more about events happening in different parts of the world. Your knowledge of the world can help you as a citizen of the community you live in.

Answers to quiz on page 69
1. kiss, 2. 18, 3. Kerry paid for everyone, 4. Spain, 5. black and purple

TABLE Manners

Table manners differ around the world. If you visit a friend's home for a **meal**, it's good to know about the **customs** they follow.

Morocco

If you are invited to a Moroccan's home, bring
5   a gift of sweet pastries, nuts, figs, dates, or flowers to the hostess.

In many traditional homes, people often sit on the floor to eat a meal.

Often, everyone shares food from the same
10   plate. The plate is put in the center of the table. Usually, everyone also drinks water from the same glass.

Only eat the food in front of you. Don't **reach** across someone for food.

15   It is common[1] to use your fingers and small pieces of bread to eat food. Use only your right hand to eat.

Don't say "no" to food. If the **host** of the meal **offers** you food or drink, take some and try a little.

Also remember: In many Moroccan homes, it is common to **take off** your shoes.

20 ## Tanzania

Tanzania is known for its fresh fish and spices. Don't act scared if your meal comes with its head still on the plate.

It is polite to try a **bite** of everything. In many Tanzanian homes, people sit at a table on small stools to eat.

25   It is OK to eat with your right hand, using bread or chapati[2] to pick up food. Everyone may take food from the same plate, but it is not usual for people to share drinks.

You may compliment the cook on a delicious meal, but don't exaggerate.[3]

In some parts of Tanzania, men and women will sit at different tables.

30   **Also remember:** It is common to take off your shoes in the home, but it is **rude** to show the bottom of your foot.

---

[1] Something that is **common** is usual or often done.
[2] **Chapati** is a kind of flat Indian bread.
[3] If you **exaggerate**, you make something seem better, larger, worse, etc. than it really is.

Reading Comprehension
Check Your Understanding

A **Choose the correct answers.**

1 Why does the writer think it is good to know about customs in other countries?
   a so you can learn the language
   b so you can order food in a restaurant
   c so you can act correctly

2 Which hand do you eat with in Morocco?
   a your left hand   b your right hand   c both hands

3 In Morocco, how do people pick up their food?
   a They use a cup.   b They use spoons.   c They use their hand.

4 Which of these should you NOT do in Tanzania?
   a show the bottom of your foot
   b eat with your hands
   c take off your shoes

B **Read the sentences below. Check (✔) true (T), false (F), or not given (NG). If the statement is false, change it to make it true.**

		T	F	NG
1	In Morocco, people wash their hands after eating.			
2	In Tanzania, people usually eat with a fork.			
3	In Morocco, a plate with food is in the center of the table.			
4	In Tanzania, it is polite to try any food that is offered to you.			

Critical Thinking

C 1 Look at the passage again. Which customs are the same in your country? Which are different?
   2 Are the table manners in your country more like Morocco's or Tanzania's?

Vocabulary Comprehension
Words in Context

A **In each sentence, (circle) the best answer. The words in blue are from the passage.**

1 For the evening meal, I had _____.
   a soup and fish   b coffee

2 Our custom is to eat lunch at 2:00 p.m., and _____ people eat lunch at that time.
   a most   b very few

3 The cup is on a high shelf. The little girl _____ reach it.
   a can   b can't

4 On the bus, it is rude to talk _____ on your cell phone.

    a loudly   **b** quietly

5 Lena was cold, so Pablo _____ his coat.

    a offered her   **b** took back

6 You are eating too fast. Take smaller _____ .

    a hosts   **b** bites

7 Simon took off his sweater because he was _____ .

    a hot   **b** cold

8 Tomoko is a great host. Everyone loves her _____ .

    a parties   **b** clothes

B **Complete the sentences below. Discuss your answers with a partner.**

    1 My favorite meal is _____ .

    2 A common custom in my country is _____ .

    3 I think it is rude to _____ .

    4 I share my house with _____ .

A **Read the paragraph below.**

Vocabulary Skill
Words for Comparing and Contrasting

Spain and Morocco share some common food and eating customs. For example, people in **both** countries eat bread with most meals. In Morocco, people often use their hands or pieces of bread to eat food. **However**, the Spanish use forks, knives, and spoons to eat most foods. In Morocco, people usually eat their largest meal in the afternoon. This is **also** true in Spain. At the end of a Spanish meal, many people have coffee. People drink coffee in Morocco, **too**, **but** not at the end of the midday meal. **Instead**, it is more common to drink sweet mint tea.

> When we compare and contrast things, we often use certain words and phrases: *both*, *also*, *too*, or *but*, *however*, and *instead*.

B **Look at the words in bold in A. Which words show that an idea is different (D)? Which show the ideas are the same (S)? Write S or D for each word.**

> _____ both   _____ however   _____ also   _____ too   _____ but   _____ instead

C **Complete the sentences with the correct word from B.**

    1 The food in the United States is not very spicy. _____ , in Mexico the food is very spicy.

    2 In _____ Taiwan and Korea, people eat rice with almost every meal.

    3 Mohammed's first language is Arabic. He _____ speaks French.

    4 When you finish eating, don't put your napkin on the plate. _____ , put it on the table.

CHAPTER 2 Homestay Diary

Before You Read
Dear Diary

A Daniela is a 22-year-old student from Brazil. She is studying in the United States. The passage on the next page is from her diary. Answer the question below.

In my opinion, studying and living in the United States would be . . .

☐ easy ☐ hard ☐ fun ☐ lonely ☐ _____

B Discuss your answer with a partner.

Reading Skill
Making Inferences

> When we read, the author does not tell us everything. Sometimes we also see new vocabulary. We can guess the author's feelings or the meaning of new words because of the information in the passage.

A Read the diary on the next page. As you read, ask yourself: How does Daniela feel?

B Complete the sentences below. (Circle) the correct answer.

1 On June 13, Daniela (was / was not) happy to be in the United States.
2 On June 25, Daniela was (angry at Valerie / unsure about what to do).
3 After talking to her friend on July 1, Daniela felt (sad / confused).
4 July 5 was a (bad / good) day for Daniela.

C What information helped you choose your answers in **B**? Underline the words in the passage. Then answer the questions on page 76.

My Homestay Diary

1 ### June 13

It's my first week in the United States and my first time in another country. So much is new and **unusual** (to me). It's great to be here. I hope I do well!

2 5 ### June 25

I live with an American host family: Valerie and Tim and their daughter, Megan. They're really nice. Every day I learn something new. For example, this morning Valerie said, "Tim and I work late, and I can't cook tonight. Help

10 yourself to anything for dinner."

3 I didn't understand Valerie. I thought she wanted help with dinner. So I bought takeout[1] for everyone. When Valerie came home, she said, "Daniela, why did you buy food? We have a lot." I explained. She said, "*Help yourself* means

15 *eat anything you want.*" I was **confused**! We laughed and ate the Chinese food anyway.

takeout Chinese food

4 ### July 1

My best friend from Brazil called today. I was really happy to talk to her, but after, I felt **kind of down**. Everything here is so different from home—the

20 food, the people, even the **weather** (It gets cold here even in the summer sometimes!).

5 ### July 5

Yesterday was Independence Day. It's a big **holiday** here. My host family had a barbecue

25 in their yard.[2] Their friends and **neighbors** came. Everyone was very friendly and **warm**. Later, I went with some friends from school to watch the fireworks. Then we went dancing. It was fun!

[1] **Takeout** is food you get at a restaurant and take home to eat.
[2] A **yard** is an open area in front of or behind a house.

Reading Comprehension
Check Your Understanding

A Choose the correct answers.

1 Where does Daniela live in the United States?
   a in a hotel   b at school   c with a family
2 Why did Daniela buy takeout?
   a She didn't understand Valerie.
   b There was no food in the house.
   c Valerie wanted to eat Chinese food.
3 On July 1, Daniela felt sad. Why?
   a She was sick.
   b Her friend was going home.
   c Things in the United States felt different.
4 On Independence Day, Daniela and her host family _____.
   a went to a parade
   b went to see the fireworks
   c had a barbeque at their house

B Read the sentences below. Check (✔) true (T), false (F), or not given (NG). If the statement is false, change it to make it true.

		T	F	NG
1	This is Daniela's second time in the U.S.			
2	In the U.S., Daniela lives with two people.			
3	July 4 is an important day in the U.S.			
4	Daniela's brother will visit her in the U.S. in August.			

Critical Thinking

C 1 Daniela is learning English while she is in the United States. What else is she learning about?
   2 Do you think Daniela's stay in the United States was mostly good? Why?

Vocabulary Comprehension
Definitions

A Match each word with its definition. The words in blue are from the passage.

1 confused _____   a kind, friendly
2 down _____   b e.g., sunny, cold, raining
3 holiday _____   c not common, different
4 kind of _____   d unsure about something
5 neighbors _____   e the people who live near you
6 unusual _____   f sad
7 warm _____   g a little
8 weather _____   h a special day when there is no work

B Complete the sentences with words in blue from **A**.

1 I read his letter twice, but I'm still _____. I don't understand it.
2 I need a coffee. I feel _____ tired.
3 Next Monday is a _____. There is no school.
4 In winter, the _____ is usually cold. But this year, December and January were very warm. That's _____.

How did your classmates benefit? Talk with two or three members of your class and ask them how the reading skill in this chapter helped them. How will they use the skill in their reading outside of the classroom? When we make connections between new things we learn and ways we can use them outside of the class, our reading improves.

Vocabulary Skill
The Prefix *un-*

A Look at the words in blue. Think about their meaning. Then match each word with its definition.

1 unable _____   **a** not the same, different
2 uneasy _____   **b** to take off paper from a gift or package
3 unfair _____   **c** deliberately not friendly
4 unkind _____   **d** cannot
5 unlike _____   **e** not calm
6 unpack _____   **f** not right, not just
7 unwrap _____   **g** to take clothes out of a suitcase

> In this chapter, you learned the word *unusual.* The prefix *un-* means *not. Un-* can come before an adjective (for example, *un + usual* = not usual, not common). Before a verb, *un-* means the opposite (for example, He locked the door. Please *unlock* it.).

B Which words from the first column in **A** are verbs? Which are adjectives? Write 1 to 7 in the correct box.

Verbs	Adjectives

C Complete each of the sentences with a word from **A**.

1 I'm going to _____ my suitcase.
2 When I talk in front of the class, I always feel _____.
3 Bill is sick. He is _____ to come to the party.
4 Do you want to _____ your birthday gifts now or after lunch?
5 Calling Mary "ugly" was very _____.
6 _____ her blonde mother, Ellen has dark hair.
7 Parent: No more video games tonight.
   Child: But that's _____! I finished my homework.

Real Life Skill

Recognizing Common Abbreviations

English uses many *abbreviations*. An abbreviation is a word made from the first letters of the name of something (for example, digital video disk = DVD). It can also be made from sounds in one word. You see these abbreviations in many places in English-speaking countries.

A Say each abbreviation below. Then match the abbreviation with its full name.

1 AC _____
2 ATM _____
3 FYI _____
4 GPA _____
5 ID _____
6 IM _____

a grade point average (a number showing your grades in school)
b instant message
c identification
d air-conditioning
e automated teller machine (to get money from a bank account)
f for your information

B Complete the sentences with the abbreviations in **A**.

1 I need some money. Let's stop at the _____.
2 Can you turn on the _____? It's hot in here.
3 With your student _____, you can see the movie for only $3.
4 In high school, Claire had a 4.0 _____. That's very good!
5 Mario sent me a(n) _____. He's going to be 20 minutes late.
6 _____ everyone: There is no class on Monday.

What do you think?

A student from another country is going to visit your country this summer. The student has some questions. Answer them with your ideas.

1 How is the weather in summer?
2 Are there special holidays or fun things to do in the summer?
3 What are two common customs in your country?
4 Tell me about meals in your country. What do people usually eat? What time do people eat?

Fluency Strategy: SQ3R

SQ3R is a simple way to help you be a better, more fluent reader and to increase your reading comprehension. **SQ3R** stands for **S**urvey, **Q**uestion, **R**ead, **R**eview, **R**ecite.

Survey

Survey is similar to the **A** in the ACTIVE approach to reading: Activate prior knowledge. When you survey, you prepare yourself by skimming quickly through the text you will read. You read the title, the headings, and the first sentence in each section of the passage. You look for and read words that are written in bold or italics. Look at any pictures and read any captions.

Look below at extracts from the passage on the next page, titled *Special Guests*.

Special Guests

Sixteen-year-old Amy Martin is on holiday with her family in San Diego, California, in the United States. They're staying at the Coronado Bay Resort Hotel. After lunch, Amy and her parents are going swimming in the hotel pool. The fourth member of their family, Martha, is going to the beach to take a surfing class. But here's the unusual thing: Martha is a dog.

At the Coronado Bay Resort, dogs and cats are special guests.

Today, there are many animal-friendly hotels around the world.

Staying at these pet-friendly hotels costs extra money.

Question

After the survey, but before you read, ask yourself questions such as *What do I want to learn as I read?* Based on your survey of *Special Guests*, write two or three questions that you hope to answer as you read.

1 _____

2 _____

3 _____

Read

After the Survey and Question stages of SQ3R, read the whole passage, *Special Guests.* Before you read, think about the 12 tips on pages 8 and 9 again.

Special Guests

1 Sixteen-year-old Amy Martin is on holiday with her family in San Diego, California, in the United States. They're staying at the Coronado Bay Resort Hotel. After lunch, Amy
5 and her parents are going swimming in the hotel pool. The fourth member of their family, Martha, is going to take a surfing class. But here's the unusual thing: Martha is a dog.

2
10 At the Coronado Bay Resort, dogs and cats are special guests. For example, Martha stays in the same room with Amy and her parents. Martha also has her own bed there. At the hotel, cooks make special meals for dogs and cats. And for fun, the animals can go surfing. There's even a surfing competition for dogs staying at the hotel.

3 15 Today, there are many animal-friendly hotels around the world. For example, at hotels in Italy and Mexico, there are dining rooms for dogs and cats where they can eat special food. And at
20 the Devon Hotel in the United Kingdom, there are special places where dogs can exercise. After that, they can relax in a private pool.

4
25 Staying at these pet-friendly hotels costs extra money. But most of the hotel guests are happy to pay a little extra to bring their pets with them. "Martha is a part of our family," says Amy Martin. "When we travel, she comes with us."

225 words   **Time taken** _____

Review

After you finish reading, review the passage. During the *review* stage of SQ3R, you review the questions that you asked yourself before reading.

A Did you find answers to your questions? Write the answers below.

1 _____

2 _____

3 _____

B Check how well you understood the passage. Choose the correct answers.

1 Who is Martha?
  a Amy's sister
  b Amy's dog
  c Amy's mother
  d Amy's surfing teacher

2 Which of the following does the Coronado Bay Resort NOT offer pets?
  a their own dining room
  b a private pool
  c surfing lessons
  d cooking classes

3 Which sentence about the Coronado Bay Resort is true?
  a You cannot bring an animal into the hotel.
  b Hotel guests must bring their own pet food.
  c Pets are treated like special guests.
  d Pets sleep in their own rooms.

4 Where can animal-friendly hotels be found?
  a around the world
  b mainly in Europe
  c mainly in the United States
  d mainly in Mexico

5 Why do people bring their pets with them on vacation?
  a They are afraid to leave the dog at home alone.
  b The animal is part of their family.
  c Animals stay free at animal-friendly hotels.
  d It is expensive to leave the dog at home.

Recite

The final step of **SQ3R** is to *recite* what you have learned while reading. Close your book and think about what you have read. You can recite in different ways.

- If you are in class, discuss what you read with a partner.
- If you are alone, write down the key information that you learned as you were reading.

SELF CHECK

Write a short answer to each of the following questions.

1 Have you ever used the SQR3 method before?

☐ Yes ☐ No ☐ I'm not sure.

2 Will you practice SQR3 in your reading outside of English class?

☐ Yes ☐ No ☐ I'm not sure.

3 Do you think SQR3 is helpful? Why or why not?

_____

_____

4 Which of the six reading passages in units 4–6 did you enjoy most? Why?

_____

_____

5 Which of the six reading passages in units 4–6 was easiest? Which was most difficult? Why?

Easiest: _____

Most difficult: _____

Why? _____

_____

6 What have you read in English outside of class recently?

_____

_____

7 What time of day is the best time for you to read and understand new ideas well? Do you use that time of day to do your most important reading and studying?

_____

_____

_____

8 How will you try to improve your reading fluency from now on?

_____

_____

Review Reading 3: World Cup Blog

Fluency Practice

Time yourself as you read through the passage. Try to read as fluently as you can. Record your time in the Reading Rate Chart on page 176. Then answer the questions on the next page.

www.sportsnews.heinle.com/worldcupblog

World Cup Blog

Qatar to Host 2022 Soccer World Cup

The tiny Middle Eastern nation of Qatar has a soccer team, but it has never played in soccer's greatest tournament, the World Cup.
5 However, something amazing will happen in 2022, when Qatar will become the first nation in the Middle East to host the men's Soccer World Cup games.

Some fans were confused about this choice. Where will the athletes
10 compete? Qatar doesn't have any stadiums built yet. Also, the weather in Qatar gets extremely hot in the summer. However, Qatar has plans to fix those problems. The country has announced plans to build enough stadiums for the tournament. To keep everyone cool, each stadium will have solar-powered air-conditioning. Qatar is also building a new airport and train
15 system. Because the stadiums will be so close together and connected by train, fans will be able to watch two games in one day.

Qatar has big plans for its new stadiums. Game officials say that after the World Cup, they will take the stadiums down. The stadiums will be taken apart and sent to countries that don't have enough money to build their own stadiums.

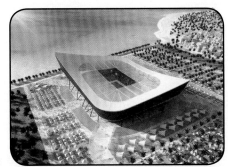

Qatar is very happy to be the first Middle Eastern nation to host the tournament. As the country's Emir, Sheikh Hamad bin Khalifa Al-Thani said to the World Cup organization, "Thank you for believing in change. . . . Thank you for giving Qatar a chance."

231 words   **Time taken** _____

Reading Comprehension

Choose the correct answer.

1 Why is it so amazing that Qatar will host the World Cup?
   a Qatar has never played in the World Cup.
   b Soccer is not played in the Middle East.
   c Qatar has very few soccer fans.
   d Qatar is a small country.

2 What is one problem that Qatar will address?
   a Their team is not good enough to compete.
   b It is very, very hot in Qatar in summer.
   c Qatar's stadiums are very far apart.
   d There is a lot of pollution in Qatar.

3 How did some soccer fans feel about the decision?
   a They thought it was strange.
   b They did not care.
   c They were very excited.
   d They were very sad.

4 What will happen to the stadiums after the World Cup in Qatar?
   a They will be used by the Qatar soccer team.
   b The stadiums will host musical concerts.
   c They will be given to other countries.
   d They will be sold to fans as souvenirs.

5 What can be inferred from the article?
   a The tournament was moved from Japan to Qatar.
   b Qatar is a wealthy country.
   c The rules of soccer will be changed in 2022.
   d Soccer is the official sport in Qatar.

Review Reading 4: Tony Wheeler of Lonely Planet

Time yourself as you read through the passage. Try to read as fluently as you can. Record your time in the Reading Rate Chart on page 176. Then answer the questions on the next page.

Tony Wheeler of Lonely Planet

1 Tony Wheeler was born to travel. His father worked for an airline, and for the first 16 years of his life, Wheeler and his family lived in many different countries.

2 5 In the early 1970s, Wheeler married a young woman named Maureen. Maureen loved to travel, too. Before settling down and getting jobs, Tony and Maureen wanted to travel. They took a year-long trip from London, through Asia, to Australia. On the trip,
10 they visited places like India, Iran, and Afghanistan.

3 When Tony and Maureen arrived in Australia, many people asked them questions about their trip. To answer these questions, Wheeler wrote a guidebook called *Across Asia on the Cheap*. The book told people about different countries—the weather,
15 customs, and places to see. But unlike travel guides in the 1970s, Wheeler's book talked about places most tourists did not go. He also wrote about unusual things to see and do. The book was very popular.

4

20 Tony and Maureen started a company called Lonely Planet. They continued traveling and wrote guidebooks for each place they visited.

5 Today, around 450 people work for Lonely Planet. The company has over 500 guidebooks, a website that shows
25 travel videos, and smartphone apps to help travelers all over the world find their way.

208 words   Time taken _____

Reading Comprehension

Choose the correct answer.

1   Who is Tony Wheeler?
    a   an airline pilot
    b   a writer
    c   a reporter
    d   a travel agent

2   Tony Wheeler's first guidebook was about his trip _____ .
    a   around the United Kingdom
    b   from Asia to England
    c   from Australia to Afghanistan
    d   from England to Australia

3   Why did Tony Wheeler write his first guidebook?
    a   He needed the money.
    b   His wife asked him to do it.
    c   Many people asked questions about his travels.
    d   He liked writing travel books.

4   How was *Across Asia on the Cheap* different from other travel guides?
    a   It was longer and more expensive.
    b   It was the first guidebook about Asia.
    c   It talked about places most tourists did not go.
    d   It told people about a country's weather, customs, and places to see.

5   Which sentence below is true?
    a   Tony Wheeler is still interested in travel.
    b   Tony Wheeler's first guidebook was not popular.
    c   After their first trip, Maureen did not travel with Tony.
    d   Today, Lonely Planet is still a small company.

Listening to Advice

Don't sleep in class.

Clean your room.

If you have a question, raise your hand.

No TV after 10:00 p.m.

When you finish eating, wash your plate.

Turn off your cell phone.

Getting Ready

Discuss these questions with a partner.

1 Look at the rules above. Which are school rules **(S)**? Which are home rules **(H)**? Write **S** or **H** on the pictures.
2 Can you think of other rules? Write two or three more rules.
3 Do you think the rules above are good? Why or why not?

CHAPTER 1 Ask Emma

Before You Read
I Need Some Advice

A **Think about answers to these questions.**

1 Read the dialog below. Amy is giving Jenna some *advice*. Do you think it is good advice?

> I want to get a part-time job, but my father says no. He says studying is more important. What can I do?

> Maybe you can finish the school term first. You can get a job in the summer or after you graduate.

2 What advice would you give Jenna? Tell a partner.

B **Look at the passage on the next page. What does Emma do? Why do people write to her? Discuss your answers with a partner.**

Reading Skill
Skimming for the Main Idea

You *skim* to get a general idea about a passage. When you skim, look quickly at the title, the photos, and the first and last sentences of each paragraph. Then you can use this general information to predict what a reading is about.

A **Look at the advice column on the next page. Who wrote the letter to Emma?**

a a teenager who has problems with his parents

b a father who has problems with his son

c a high school student who has problems with his school

B **What advice do you think Emma will give? Complete the sentence with your ideas.**

I think Emma will tell him to _____

_____.

C **Now read the passage closely. Were your answers in A and B correct? Answer the questions on page 90.**

Do you need help with a problem? Ask Emma!

Dear Emma,
I have a problem, and I need your help. My parents are really **strict** and never let me do anything! For example, when I **go out** with
5 my friends, my mom always asks, "Where are you going? Who are you going with?" Two months ago, I got an earring, and my father was really angry. He made me take it out.[1] My parents want to **control** *everything* I do. But I'm
10 18 years old!
I try to talk to my mom and dad,[2] but they don't listen. They say, "This is our house, and these are our **rules**." Then we have a fight. Why is it so hard for them to understand me?

15 Josh

Dear Josh,
You asked, "Why is it so hard for them to understand me?" That's a good question. You're **growing up**, but often it's hard for your parents to see this. To them, you are still a **child** and they want to **protect** you.
20 Sometimes, it's hard to talk to your parents. Here's an idea: Write your mother and father a letter. Explain your feelings calmly. In the letter, **describe** your friends. Tell your parents about yourself and your life, too. Then maybe they will understand you better. After your parents read the letter, try to talk to them.
I hope this helps!

25 Emma

[1] If you **take** something **out**, you remove it.
[2] Your **mom** and **dad** are your mother and father.

Reading Comprehension
Check Your Understanding

A Choose the correct answers.

1 What is Josh's biggest problem with his parents?
  a They want to know where he goes.
  b They are too strict.
  c They don't like his earring.

2 Josh says his parents never _____ to him.
  a talk   b listen   c give anything

3 Emma tells Josh to _____ to his parents first.
  a write a letter   b talk   c listen

4 Which of the following would Emma most likely agree with?
  a Josh is still a child.
  b Emma should write to Josh's parents to explain things.
  c Josh's parents need to change how they see Josh.

B What advice did Emma give Josh? Complete the sentence below with the correct answer(s).

In the letter to his parents, Josh should write about _____.
☐ his friends   ☐ his childhood   ☐ his feelings   ☐ himself and his life

Critical Thinking

C 1 Do you agree with Emma's advice to Josh? Why?
  2 What other advice would you give Josh?

Make connections beyond the classroom. How could you use the information that you have learned from this passage outside of the classroom? When you make connections beyond the classroom it makes reading more enjoyable.

Vocabulary Comprehension
Words in Context

A In each sentence, circle the best answer. The words in blue are from the passage.

1 Our teacher is strict. If you miss two classes, _____.
  a it's no problem   b you fail the course

2 If you go out, you _____ your house.
  a leave   b enter

3 My parents try to control me. I can only do _____.
  a what I want   b what they want

4 Which one is a rule?
  a This store is open 24 hours.   b Do not eat or drink in the library.

5 Anna is a child. She's _____.
  a 11   b 28

6 When a person grows up, he gets _____.
  a angry   b older

7 To protect your eyes from the sun, _____ your sunglasses.

    a wear   **b** take off

8 If you describe something, you _____ it.

    a explain   **b** forget

B **Answer the questions below. Discuss your answers with a partner.**

  1 Describe your parents. Are they strict? Are there many rules in your house?

  2 When you grow up, do you want to be like your parents?

A **Look at the blue word in the sentence below. The circled words help you understand its meaning.**

> Jo's parents are very easygoing. They (never get angry) with her.
> **Part of speech:** _adjective_
> **Meaning:**   ☐ strict   ☑ relaxed, calm

To understand the meaning of the underlined word . . .

* think about the word's part of speech (noun, verb, adjective, or adverb).
* look at the circled words. They can help you understand the word's meaning.

B **Read the sentences below. Pay attention to the blue words. Write the word's part of speech (noun, verb, adjective). Then check (✓) the word's meaning.**

  1 Josh always argues with his parents. They never agree.

      Part of speech: _____

      Meaning: ☐ understand   ☐ fights

  2 When you talk to your parents, explain your feelings. Tell them what you think.

      Part of speech: _____

      Meaning: ☐ thoughts and opinions   ☐ plans for the future

  3 Don't lie to your parents. Always tell the truth.

      Part of speech: _____

      Meaning: ☐ say something not true   ☐ say something true

  4 Talk to your parents patiently. Don't yell.

      Part of speech: _____

      Meaning: ☐ calmly   ☐ angrily

C **Which words in the sentences in B helped you understand the meaning? (Circle) them.**

Vocabulary Skill

Guessing Vocabulary Meaning from Context

Sometimes you can guess the meaning of new vocabulary. Think about the word's part of speech (noun, verb, adjective, or adverb). You can also use other words in the sentence to help you understand the new word.

CHAPTER 2 Peer Pressure

Before You Read
Under Pressure

A Think about answers to these questions.

1 Who is your best friend? How are you similar? How are you different?
2 Are your friends' opinions important to you?
3 Read the sentence below. Is the word *pressure* positive or negative?

> There is a lot of **pressure** to pass the university entrance exam. It's hard for students.

B Discuss your answers with a partner.

Reading Skill
Making and Checking Predictions

> When you read, you can often *predict* what will come next. While you read, you also check to see if your predictions were correct. Good readers learn to make and check their predictions.

A Read lines 1–11 in the passage on the next page. Then stop and answer the questions below.

1 Where are Alicia, Nina, and Vicki?

_____

2 Why do Nina and Vicki laugh at Alicia?

_____

3 What do you think Alicia will do next?

_____

B Now read lines 12–23. Then stop and answer the questions below.

1 Were your predictions in **A** correct? _____

2 What do you think Alicia will do next? _____

_____

C Now read lines 24–25. Was your prediction in **B** correct? Read the whole passage again. Then answer the questions on page 94.

Your Turn to Talk

This week's topic: peer[1] **pressure**

It's the week before school starts. Alicia Gonzalez is shopping for clothes with two friends, Nina and
5 Vicki. Alicia **puts on** a black jacket, turns to her friends, and says, "Hey, what do you think?"

The girls look at her and both start laughing. "No way, Alicia!"

10 Nina laughs. "That's a guy's[2] jacket."

Alicia **frowns** angrily. "Yeah, well . . . *I* like it."

"Yeah," says Vicki, "but what will people at school say?"

Alicia thinks for a moment. Then she takes off the jacket. "Yeah, you're right."

Peer pressure. We all know about it. Your friends wear certain clothes or
15 listen to certain music. You don't want to be different. So you do those things, too.

Fifteen minutes later, Alicia is still thinking about the black jacket. "Yeah, there's pressure to follow the **crowd**," she explains. "If your clothes or hair are different, people **make fun of** you. You know, they laugh and point."

20 Vicki agrees. "It's true. You even have to have a certain kind of boyfriend or girlfriend! I think these *rules* are **childish**. But when you're different, you feel like an **outsider**. And that's hard."

Alicia walks away. "Hey Alicia," calls Nina. "Where are you going?"

"To get the black jacket. I don't **care about** what others think. I like it, and I'm
25 buying it."

---

[1] Your **peers** are people the same age as you.
[2] A **guy** is a man.

Reading Comprehension
Check Your Understanding

A Choose the correct answers.

1 What do Alicia's friends think of the black jacket?
   a They like it.   b They think it is OK   c They don't like it.

2 Why does Alicia take off the black jacket?
   a She doesn't like the color.
   b It's too expensive.
   c She's worried about her friends' opinions.

3 What is the meaning of **peer pressure** (line 14)?
   a You want to be like your friends, so you do what they do.
   b You want to be different from your friends and classmates.
   c You want to help your friends.

4 At the end, Alicia _____ .
   a doesn't buy the jacket
   b buys the jacket
   c hasn't decided whether to buy the jacket or not

B Complete the sentence about peer pressure. Choose the correct answer(s).

The passage says for many people, there is pressure to _____ .
☐ wear certain clothes   ☐ listen to certain music
☐ get a part-time job   ☐ have a certain type of boyfriend or girlfriend

Critical Thinking

C 1 Think about the peer pressure Alicia and her friends feel. Do you ever feel this?
   2 When Alicia wears the black jacket to school, what do you think will happen?

Vocabulary Comprehension
Words in Context

A Read the sentences below. Check (✓) true (T) or false (F). If the statement is false, change it to make it true. The words in blue are from the passage.

		T	F
1	A big group of people is called a crowd.		
2	You put on a coat when you enter your house.		
3	You frown when you are happy.		
4	If you feel a lot of pressure at school, you feel good.		
5	If you make fun of someone, you laugh at them and say unkind things.		
6	Phil is very childish. This means he's serious.		
7	An outsider is someone who is the same as everyone else.		
8	If you care about something, it is important to you.		

B Complete each sentence with a word in blue from **A**.

1　I _____ my grades, so I study a lot.
2　Lena is ten and very tall and skinny. The children in her class often _____ her.
3　Don't get angry over losing the game. It's _____ .
4　Please _____ a sweater. It's cold this morning.

A Complete the sentences below with the *-ish* form of the noun in parentheses.

1　My favorite TV show is a _____ (Britain) comedy.
2　Ron only thinks about himself. He is so _____ (self)!
3　Linnea is half _____ (Sweden) and half _____ (Ireland).
4　Koji is 35, but he has a _____ (boy) face.
5　Jan likes _____ (Turkey) coffee, but I prefer _____ (England) tea.
6　My grandmother is 85, but she still has a _____ (girl) laugh.

B Complete the questions with an *-ish* adjective.

1　Do you ever watch movies or TV shows in _____?
2　Do you know someone who is _____?
3　Are you _____?

C Ask a partner your questions from **B** or write your own answers.

Vocabulary Skill
The Suffix *–ish*

In this chapter, you learned the adjective *childish*. The suffix *-ish* means *like* (*child + ish* = like a child). The suffix *-ish* is also used to describe nationality or something from a certain country (for example, *Spanish*).

Real Life Skill
Understanding Written Signs

In many public places, it is common to see signs that tell us what we can or cannot do.

A Do you ever see signs written in English? If yes, where? What do the signs say?

B The rules below come from English signs. Where would you see each sign? Match each rule with a photo.

1 CANS AND GLASS BOTTLES ONLY
2 CAUTION: Children crossing. Drive slow.
3 KEEP DOG ON LEASH
4 NO ONE UNDER 21 ALLOWED
5 Passengers only beyond this point.
6 Take a number. Wait your turn.

What do you think?

1 Read the two situations below. What advice can you give each person?
   Situation 1: Your sister has a boyfriend who she really likes. But your parents don't like him at all, and want her to stop seeing him. What can she do?
   Situation 2: Your friend Ben is shy and a bit of an outsider. At school, many people make fun of him. What can he do?
2 Do you always follow the rules at school, at home, or at work? If you don't, what happens?

Reward yourself. Review your progress over the past few units. How have you improved as a reader? What do you still need to work on? If you are achieving your goals, reward yourself. The reward might be a special dinner with friends or a new book to read.

Remarkable People

Jeanne Calment lived to be 122 years old. She met Vincent van Gogh.

Lionel Messi is a famous soccer player. He has started a charity[1] for children.

Chen Shu-chu (right) is a vegetable seller who doesn't earn much money, but has given a lot to charity.

Nick Vujicic was born without arms and legs. He travels the world inspiring people, especially teenagers, to love themselves and live life with joy.

Getting Ready

Discuss these questions with a partner.
1 Look at the photos. Which people do you know?
2 The title of this unit is *Remarkable People*. Why are the people in the photos special?
3 In your opinion, which person is the most remarkable? Why?

[1] A **charity** is a group that raises money to help people.

CHAPTER 1 A Real Life Superhero

Before You Read
What are you afraid of?

A Think about answers to these questions.

1 Read the sentence below. Then complete the second sentence to make it true for you.

> I'm **afraid of** spiders. They make me very scared!

I'm afraid of . . .
☐ spiders   ☐ heights (high places)
☐ the dark   ☐ _____

2 Look at the title of the passage and the photo on the next page. What is the man doing? What do you think this passage is about?

B Discuss your answers with a partner.

Reading Skill
Understanding the Order of Events

> Some passages tell us about an order of events. You often see dates, numbers, words, and phrases about time: *one day, still, later, then, today*. These words help you understand when something happened.

A Read the sentences below. Then put the events in the correct order from 1–5.

The Story of Alain Robert

_1_ **a** One day, Alain Robert returned home from school.

____ **b** He decided to climb the apartment building. He entered his house through an open window.

____ **c** Then in 2011, he climbed the Burj Khalifa tower in Dubai.

____ **d** Today, Robert still climbs buildings. In 2004, he climbed a building in Taipei.

____ **e** He didn't have his keys and couldn't enter his apartment.

B Quickly read the passage on the next page. Are your answers in **A** correct?

C Now read the passage closely. Then answer the questions on page 100.

Set your reading rate goal. As you prepare to read, set a reading rate goal. Use your data from the charts at the end of the book. Based on your previous performance, how many words-per-minute do you think you can read now? Time yourself and practice over and over until you've reached your goal.

A Real Life Superhero

Alain Robert climbs Burj Khalifa (828 meters) in Dubai.

As a child, Alain Robert was **afraid** of heights. One day, when he was 12, he returned home from school. At the front door of his building, he **looked for** his keys. He didn't have them. It was 3:30, and his parents worked until 6:00 p.m. Robert looked at his apartment on the eighth floor. He saw an open window. He closed his eyes and
5   pictured himself **climbing** the building. When he opened his eyes, he told himself, "I can do it." Fifteen minutes later, he was in his house, and his **fear** of heights was gone.

Today, Robert (a **native** of France) still climbs buildings. In 2004, he climbed Taipei 101 (the tallest building in the world at the time), and in 2011 he climbed the Burj Khalifa tower in Dubai. To **reach** the top of a building, Robert usually uses
10 only his hands and special shoes. To climb the Burj Khalifa tower, though, he was made to wear safety ropes.

Robert climbs as a hobby. He also does it to make money for charity (for children and the homeless[1]). When he climbs, he wants to send a message to people. If you have a dream—something you really want to do—it can become real. But you
15 must be **brave** and keep trying. If something bad happens, don't **give up**. Close your eyes and tell yourself, "I can do it."

---

[1] **The homeless** are people who don't have homes.

Reading Comprehension
Check Your Understanding

A **Choose the correct answers.**

1 What is the main idea of this passage?
 a Climbing buildings is easy.
 b Robert is afraid of heights.
 c You can control your fears.

2 When Robert climbs a building, he usually uses _____.
 a special tools
 b his hands and special shoes
 c his hands only

3 Robert climbs for two reasons. What are they?
 a for fun and for his health
 b for charity and for his job
 c for charity and for fun

4 If you feel afraid of doing something, what is Robert's advice?
 a Tell yourself: "I can do it."
 b Practice doing it alone first.
 c Find something else you love to do.

B **Read each pair of sentences. Which event happened first, a or b? Check (✔) your answer.**

1 ☐ **a** Robert looked for his keys.
  ☐ **b** Robert looked at his apartment.

2 ☐ **a** Robert closed his eyes.
  ☐ **b** Robert saw an open window.

3 ☐ **a** Robert's fear of heights was gone.
  ☐ **b** Robert imagined climbing the building.

4 ☐ **a** Robert climbed a building in Dubai.
  ☐ **b** Robert climbed Taipei 101.

Critical Thinking

C **1** What do you think about Robert? Why?
 2 At the end of the passage, Robert gives some advice. What is it? Do you agree with this advice?

A Read the sentences below. Check (✔) true (T) or false (F). If the statement is false, change it to make it true. The words in blue are from the passage.

		T	F
1	If you are afraid of something, you like it.		
2	You look for your wallet if you can't find it.		
3	If you climb a tree, you go down.		
4	Fear is a good feeling.		
5	If you are native to a place, you have just moved there.		
6	If you reach a place, you arrive there.		
7	If you give up smoking, you start smoking.		
8	A brave person is afraid of many things.		

B Complete the sentences below with your ideas. Discuss your answers with a partner.

1 I think _____ is a brave person because _____ .

2 Something that I'd like to give up is _____ .

3 When I am afraid of something, I usually _____ .

A Read the sentences below. Circle the words that are synonyms for the blue words.

1 As a child, Robert was afraid of heights. His friends went rock climbing, but he didn't go. He was too scared.

2 Robert looked for his keys. He searched his backpack and his jacket, but he couldn't find them.

3 When Robert climbs, he uses no rope. This is not safe. "Yes, it's dangerous," he says, "but it is also interesting."

4 Once, Robert fell 15 meters. The doctors said, "You must stop climbing." But he didn't quit.

> *Synonyms* are words with similar or the same meanings (for example, *like* and *enjoy*). Learning synonyms is a good way to increase your vocabulary and improve your writing.

B Complete the sentences below with a circled word from A. You might have to change the form of the word or phrase.

1 Don't drive so fast in this rain. It's _____!

2 My father _____ smoking two months ago.

3 Tom: Mary, what are you doing?
   Mary: I'm _____ for my glasses. I can't find them.

4 Carlos is very brave. He's not _____ of anything.

CHAPTER 2 The Tiffin Men

Before You Read
What's for lunch?

A **Think about answers to these questions.**

1 Do you bring your lunch to school or work, or do you eat at a restaurant?
2 Look at the passage on the next page and answer the questions.
   a What do you know about India? Can you name any Indian cities?
   b Look at the photo and the word in the search box. What do you think a *dabbawallah* is?

B **Discuss your answers with a partner.**

Reading Skill
Scanning

You *scan* to find information fast. When you scan, you only look for the information you need (words or numbers). You don't read every word.

A **Read the questions and answers below.**

1 What do the dabbawallahs do?
   a They work in restaurants.   b They deliver lunches.
2 What is another name for the dabbawallahs?
   a the Mumbai Men   b the Tiffin Men
3 How many dabbawallahs are there?
   a 5,000   b 200,000
4 Which sentence about the dabbawallahs is true?
   a They are poor.   b They like to read.
5 What do some dabbawallahs also do?
   a They teach classes.   b They work in companies.

B **Now scan the passage on the next page to find answers to the questions in A.**

C **Look at the question at the start of the passage. Discuss with a partner. Use your answers in A.**

D **Now read the whole passage. Then answer the questions on page 104.**

Your Questions Answered!

You have questions? We have the answers!

Type your question here: Who are the dabbawallahs of India?

Dabbawallah: from Hindi[1] meaning *lunchbox deliveryman*. Dabbawallahs are sometimes also called *Tiffin Men*.

Description

5 It's lunchtime in Mumbai, India (population: 12 million), and students and businesspeople around the city have to make a choice. Should they go to a restaurant or eat a hot lunch from home? 10 Today, many can choose the second **option**, thanks to[2] the dabbawallahs.

Every day, 5,000 dabbawallahs **deliver** 200,000 lunches to people all over Mumbai. The dabbawallahs work together. They **pick up** a person's lunch from his or her house (or a 15 restaurant). They put the hot lunch in a special box (called a *tiffin*). Then they bring the lunch to the person's office or school by lunch time. The men travel long **distances** (many kilometers a day) on bicycle, train, and foot to deliver the lunchboxes on time.

a tiffin

20 Many of the deliverymen are poor. Most cannot read. They use a special **system** of colors and lines to write a person's name and address on a lunchbox.

There are many **challenges** (traffic,[3] bad weather, long distances), but the men are very **organized**. On average, for every 6 million lunches they deliver, they make fewer than one **mistake**! The dabbawallahs do so well that some teach classes at business schools 25 around the world!

PRINT | EMAIL PAGE | MORE INFORMATION ON THIS TOPIC

---

[1] **Hindi** is one of the official languages of India.
[2] If something happens **thanks to** a person or thing, it happens because of that person or thing.
[3] **Traffic** refers to all the cars, etc. on the roads in a particular area.

Reading Comprehension
Check Your Understanding

A **Choose the correct answers.**

1 The dabbawallahs _____.
  a make a person's lunch at home
  b cook food at a restaurant
  c pick up a person's lunch from their house

2 The dabbawallahs use colors and lines to show a person's name and address on their lunchbox. Why?
  a It's fast and easy.
  b They cannot read.
  c Their boss tells them to.

3 When the dabbawallahs deliver lunches, which problem do they NOT usually have?
  a traffic   **b** long distances   **c** wrong addresses

4 The dabbawallahs make _____ mistakes.
  a no   **b** very few   **c** a lot of

B **Read the sentences below. Check (✔) true (T) or false (F). If the statement is false, change it to make it true.**

		T	F
1	Mumbai is a city with two million people.		
2	The dabbawallahs deliver lunches by car.		
3	Every day, the dabbawallahs deliver 10,000 lunches.		
4	Some dabbawallahs teach business classes.		

Critical Thinking

C **1** In your opinion, are the dabbawallahs remarkable people? Why or why not?
      2 Are there people like the dabbawallahs in your country? What do they do?

Vocabulary Comprehension
Words in Context

A **In each sentence, (circle) the best answer. The words in blue are from the passage.**

1 The mail carrier delivers mail to your house. This means he or she _____ your mail.
  a brings   **b** takes away

2 Simone picks up her children after school. This means she _____ school.
  a takes the children from   **b** brings the children to

3 It's a long distance from Spain to _____.
  a France   **b** Japan

4 There is a system for finding a word in a dictionary. All words are listed _____.
  a from A to Z   **b** in any order

5 Reading a book _____ is a challenge for many people.
  a in another language   **b** in your own language

6 On Kim's desk, there are papers and books in a mess. She
_____ an organized person.

    a is   **b** is not

7 On the plane, there are two options for dinner: chicken or beef.
You have two _____.

    a ideas   **b** choices

8 If you make a mistake, you do something _____.

    a right   **b** wrong

B **Answer the questions below. Discuss your answers with a partner.**

1 Do you make many mistakes in English?

_____

2 Are you an organized person? Give an example to show why or why not.

_____

3 What is something that is a challenge for you to do?

_____

4 What is the distance between your house and your school?

_____

Vocabulary Skill
make + noun

A **Read the dialog below. <u>Underline</u> the phrases that use the word *make*.**

Nadia: Jill, can I use your cell phone? I need to make a call. I want to make plans for dinner.

Manolo: Hello?

Nadia: Hi, Manolo. It's Nadia. What do you want to do for dinner tonight? We need to make a decision.

Manolo: We can go to the new Thai restaurant on 24th Street.

Nadia: OK, I'll make a reservation.

Manolo: Or we can make dinner at home. It's less expensive. I'll cook.

> In this chapter, you read the phrases *make a mistake* and *make a choice*. In English, the verb *make* goes with many nouns.

B **Complete the sentences below with a phrase with *make* from A.**

1 Call the restaurant and _____ for four people at 7:30.

2 If you need to _____, there's a pay phone on the first floor.

3 It's very difficult to _____ with Sue. She's always busy.

4 Do you want to _____ or go out to eat tonight?

5 Please _____: do you want to have Japanese or Korean food tonight?

> **Importance of vocabulary skill development.** As you practice vocabulary skills you will find you understand new words more easily. This will help you learn more vocabulary on your own.

Real Life Skill
Doing Research Online

We use the Internet to find information. When you search for information, you can type a question (*Who is Alain Robert?*) or keywords (*Alain Robert climb*). Then you can scan a page to find the information.

A **Imagine you need information about a famous person (for example, when and where Shakespeare was born). What websites could you use? Write your ideas below.**

www.google.com _____ _____

B **J. K. Rowling wrote the *Harry Potter* books. Find more information about her.**

- Go to a website in **A**.
- Type the keywords written in the chart.
- Scan the webpages quickly to find answers.
- Write the answers you find in the chart.
- Write the website where you find the answers.

Keywords	Website (Source)	Answer
J. K. Rowling birth date		
J. K. Rowling birthplace		
J. K. Rowling fan mail address		

C **Find one more fact about J. K. Rowling. Write it below.**

_____

D **Use the information from B and C and write a paragraph about J. K. Rowling. Include the following information:**

- What does J. K. Rowling do and why is she famous?
- Where and when was J. K. Rowling born?
- Where can you write to J. K. Rowling?
- one more fact about her

What do you think?

Name a remarkable person. The person can be alive now or may have lived in the past. In your opinion, why is (or was) this person incredible?

That's Entertainment

Nicholas Sparks, writer famous for *Dear John* and *The Last Song*

Charice, a singer originally from the Philippines. She's a TV actress, too!

Matt Damon, American actor

Heidi Klum, model and TV host, and singer Seal.

Getting Ready

Discuss these questions with a partner.
1 Look at the photos above. Do you know these people?
2 Who are the most popular celebrities in your country? Are they actors, singers, talk-show hosts, or writers?
3 Who are your favorite entertainers?

CHAPTER 1 Artists in Two Languages

Before You Read
Learning Another Language

A **Think about answers to these questions.**

1 What is the hardest part of learning another language?
2 Look at the names and photos on the next page. What do you know about these entertainers? Where are they from? What are their first languages? Do you know any of their movies or songs?

B **Discuss your answers with a partner.**

Reading Skill
Understanding Cause and Effect

Effects tell us *what happened* and causes tell us *why*. When you read, pay attention to words like *because*, *since*, *as a result*, and *so*. These words can help you understand causes and effects.

A **Look quickly at the passage on the next page. Read the title and the headings. Then answer the question below.**

What is this passage about?
a Jay Chou's and Shakira's favorite movies
b how Jay Chou and Shakira learned English
c why Jay Chou and Shakira are successful

B **Read the questions. Then quickly scan the passage to find the answers.**

1 Why did Shakira start writing songs in English?
 a She liked to sing songs in English.
 b She wanted to keep control of her music.
 c She wanted her songs to be more popular.
2 Why did Shakira read newspapers and poetry in English?
 a to learn to express her feelings
 b to be more popular
 c because they were interesting
3 Why was the movie *The Green Hornet* difficult for Jay Chou?
 a He only spoke a little English.
 b It was his first movie.
 c He didn't like New York.
4 How did Jay improve his English?
 a He read a lot of books.
 b He watched television shows.
 c He practiced with other actors.
5 What does Jay want to do in the future?
 a write songs in English
 b act in more movies
 c work with Seth Rogan again

C **Read the passage on the next page. Then answer the questions on page 110.**

ARTISTS IN TWO LANGUAGES

Shakira

First album in English: *Laundry Service*

5 **How she learned English:** Many people wanted to translate Shakira's songs from Spanish to English. Shakira agreed, but she felt nervous about losing control of her music. So 10 she decided to write her own songs in English.

Shakira studied grammar and common **expressions**. She started reading newspapers and **poetry** because 15 she wanted to know how people use English to express their feelings.

Biggest challenge: Writing her first songs in English. Today, Shakira writes and performs her music in 20 Spanish and English for fans around the world. In the summer of 2010, Shakira was selected to record and **perform** the theme song for the World Cup in South Africa, called 25 "Waka Waka (This Time for Africa)."

Jay Chou

First film in English: *The Green Hornet*

How he learned English: Jay spoke 30 very little English before he got his **role** in *The Green Hornet*. He practiced every day for more than a month. At first he said all of his lines phonetically,[1] but soon, Jay's English 35 improved. He was able to speak English and talk with his costars. His English was not perfect, but he got **compliments** from the other actors.

Language exchange: As they shot[2] 40 the movie, Jay and his costar Seth Rogan took turns teaching each other Chinese and English.

Language crossover: Jay is an award-winning singer, but all of his 45 **current** songs are Chinese. He hopes that in the future he can write songs in English as well.

---

[1] If you say something **phonetically**, you say it by making its sounds, without necessarily knowing the meaning.
[2] When you **shoot** a movie, you make one, using a camera.

Reading Comprehension
Check Your Understanding

A **Choose the correct answers.**

1 At first, _____ in English was difficult for Shakira.
   a singing   **b** songwriting   **c** speaking

2 How often does Shakira use English in her music today?
   a never   **b** rarely   **c** often

3 Why did Jay say his lines phonetically at first?
   a He wanted to sound cool.
   b He was still learning English.
   c He didn't want to remember his lines.

4 What did Jay teach Seth Rogan to do?
   a cook Chinese food   **b** speak Chinese   **c** sing Chinese songs

B **How did Shakira and Jay improve their English? Read the phrases below. Then complete the chart.**

> **a** read poetry   **b** studied grammar   **c** studied phonetically
> **d** practiced speaking with his costars   **e** read the newspaper
> **f** learned common expressions

Shakira
Jay Chou

Critical Thinking

C **1** Look at the ways of learning English in **B** above. Do you ever do these things? Do they help you? Why?

2 What were the biggest challenges for Shakira and Jay Chou? Do you ever have these problems?

Vocabulary Comprehension
Definitions

A **Match each word with its definition. The words in blue are from the passage.**

1 compliment _____   **a** a movie

2 current _____   **b** to tell someone you like something about them

3 exchange _____   **c** to sing, act, play music for people

4 expression _____   **d** to give something and get something back, to trade

5 film _____   **e** an actor's character in a movie

6 perform _____   **f** a common saying in a language (for example, *What's up?*)

7 poetry _____   **g** writing in which the words are chosen for their beauty and sound

8 role _____   **h** happening now

B Answer the questions below. Discuss your answers with a partner.

1   What are two common expressions in your language? What do they mean in English?

   _____

   _____

2   Who is your favorite actor? What is the actor's best film? What is the actor's role in the film?

   _____

   _____

A Put the adjectives in the correct place in the chart. You already know some of the adjectives. Use your dictionary to understand the new words.

afraid	bored	calm	confused	energized	grumpy
happy	hopeful	inspired	lazy	nervous	scared

Positive feelings	Negative feelings
	afraid/scared

Vocabulary Skill
Feelings

This chapter's passage tells us that both Jay Chou and Shakira felt *uneasy* when they first acted or sang in English. There are many adjectives in English to describe how a person feels.

B Add one more positive and one more negative feeling to the list. Use your dictionary to help you find the words in English.

C Discuss the questions below with a partner.

1   When you feel nervous, what do you do to feel calmer?
2   When you wake up in the morning, are you grumpy?
3   How do you feel today? Choose a word from **A** or **B**. If your feeling is negative, how can you change it to feel better?

Reading helps you learn. A famous American writer, David McCullough, has said, "A good way to learn is to read books." When we read, we learn about ideas that others have. It is important to read widely so that we learn about a variety of opinions on a single topic. You will learn more as you read more!

Before You Read
What a great show!

A Match each type of dancer in the box with a picture. Then think about answers to the questions below.

> acrobat   ballroom dancer   ballerina   modern dancer

a _____   b _____   c _____   d _____

1 What things do these performers have in common? What are some differences?

2 Look quickly at the passage on the next page. Do you know anything about modern dance?

B Discuss your answers with a partner.

Reading Skill
Understanding Main Ideas

> In a good paragraph, the first sentence introduces an idea. This is often called a *topic sentence*. Each sentence after the topic sentence should support the first idea.

A Read the passage on the next page.

B Do the topic sentences introduce ideas? Do the sentences after each topic sentence support the idea? How?

C Read the passage again. Then answer the questions on page 114.

> **Why are you learning English?** Think about why you are learning English. Why is learning to read better in English important to you? Keeping these reasons in mind will help you as you complete this chapter.

www.heinle.com/pilobolus

What a great show!

Last night I saw the most amazing **performance**. The modern dance company[1] Pilobolus was performing **live** at my sister's
5 university. She bought tickets so she and I could go.

I was curious about the show. Some of my friends practice ballet or hip hop, but my sister said that Pilobolus
10 would be very different from those kinds of dances. She was right.

You should have seen the dancers! The Pilobolus dancers appeared on the **stage** in brightly colored costumes.[2] They moved together in such an amazing way. They were also very strong. It must be hard to **lift**, jump, and carry other
15 dancers across the stage. I don't think I could carry someone and still be as **graceful** as they are!

The Pilobolus dancers are very **flexible**. They **create** shapes and shadows with their bodies. I heard a woman say that Pilobolus dancers remind her of sculptures.

I feel like I learned so much about dance in just one night. Pilobolus has created more than 100 **original** dances. I hope to see another one of their shows soon.

[1] A **dance company** is a group of dancers who work together.
[2] A **costume** is the clothing that a performer wears.

Reading Comprehension
Check Your Understanding

A Choose the correct answers.

1 What is true about the writer?
   a She studied dance in college.
   b She is a hip hop dancer.
   c She saw a dance performance.
2 How does the writer describe the dancers' movements?
   a difficult b easy c boring
3 What does the writer say about the dancers?
   a They could bend their bodies very easily.
   b They made many mistakes when dancing.
   c They were mostly women.
4 Which of these statements is true?
   a The writer has seen many of Pilobolus' shows.
   b The Pilobolus group performs many different dances.
   c The writer's sister thought the dancers looked like sculptures.

B In the passage, the writer uses the adjectives in blue to describe the Pilobolus dancers and their show. Write some words that can go with each adjective. Discuss your ideas with a partner.

Example: creative _____*painter*_____
1 amazing _____
2 strong _____
3 graceful _____
4 flexible _____
5 original _____

Critical Thinking

C 1 Which do you think is more fun: watching something new and exciting or creating something new and exciting? Why?
2 Do you think being a modern dancer would be fun? Why?

Vocabulary Comprehension
Odd Word Out

A For each group of words, (circle) the word that does not belong. The words in blue are from the passage.

1 first   reused   original
2 live   on video   on CD
3 discussion   performance   conversation
4 create   make   break
5 window   floor   stage
6 stiff   flexible   bendable
7 graceful   clumsy   smooth
8 drop   lift   fall

B **Answer the questions below. Discuss your answers with a partner.**

1 What's your favorite play, movie, or dance? Who created it?

_____

2 Do you lift weights for exercise? Why?

_____

3 Are you a graceful person?

_____

4 Do you like to go to modern art performances?

_____

A **Read the two sentences below aloud. What part of speech (noun, verb, adjective, adverb) is the word _live_?**

live (this word rhymes with _give_): I _live_ in Tokyo.
live (this words rhymes with _dive_): I love to go to performances and see artists _live_.

B **Read each pair of sentences. For each word in blue, write the part of speech. Then match the sentence with the correct definition.**

Vocabulary Skill
Homographs

> _Homographs_ are words that are spelled the same but pronounced differently. They also have different meanings.

1 (close: **a** near   **b** the opposite of open)

The door is open. Please close it.
part of speech _____   definition _____

I live very close to school.
part of speech _____   definition _____

2 (wind: **a** turn   **b** air moving)

There is a strong wind today.
part of speech _____   definition _____

For this clock to work, you must wind it.
part of speech _____   definition _____

3 (present: **a** gift   **b** give)

I gave Tim a present for his birthday.
part of speech _____   definition _____

Tomorrow, I must present my paper to the teacher.
part of speech _____   definition _____

C **Ask your teacher how the words in B are pronounced. Then read the sentences aloud with a partner.**

Real Life Skill

Understanding Movie Ratings

In many countries, movies are rated. A letter or number shows if a movie is OK for young children, teenagers, or adults only. For example, *Rated G* in the United States or *U* in Britain means a movie is OK for all ages.

A **In your country, are movies rated? What different ratings are used?**

B **Look at the chart. These are American movie ratings. Are the ratings in your country the same? Discuss with a partner.**

G	General
PG	Parental guidance
PG-13	Parental guidance for children under 13
R	Restricted (Under 17 requires accompanying parent or adult guardian)
NC-17	No children under 17

C **Look at the movie titles and ratings in the box. Answer the questions below.**

Inception, Rated PG-13   *Saw*, Rated NC-17
Toy Story 3, Rated G   *The Girl with the Dragon Tattoo*, Rated R

1 Which movie(s) can you see?

_____

2 Which movie(s) are OK for a three-year-old to see?

_____

3 Which movie(s) can a 14-year-old see?

_____

What do you think?

1 What special abilities do you have? For example, are you a good singer? Can you act, paint, draw, write well, or play a musical instrument?

2 What do you want to learn to do: paint, act, sing, draw, write well, play a musical instrument, or something else?

Complete the sentence below.

I want to learn to _____ because _____.

Fluency Strategy: Dealing with Unknown Words

If you stop to learn every new word you read, you will read less fluently. It is often possible to skip unknown words when you read.

Unknown Words

A Read the first letter of the passage *Help Me Train My Pet* on the next page. <u>Underline</u> any words you do not know. After you underline the words, don't stop—keep reading!

B Look at the words that you underlined in the paragraphs above. Complete the chart below.

Unknown word	Line number	Unknown word	Line number

Did you underline any word more than once? If a new word comes up many times, then it may be important to learn that word. For example, the word *naughty* appears twice in the first paragraph. Do you already know what *naughty* means? If not, can you guess its meaning?

C Now answer this comprehension question about the paragraphs you just read:

1 What does Joan want to know?
   a where to buy a new cat
   b why her cat is being bad
   c why her dog hates her cat
   d what she should name her cat

Were you able to answer this question without looking up the meaning of the unknown word(s)? Remember, you don't always need to understand every word to understand the meaning of the passage.

D Now read the whole passage on the next page, without using a dictionary. <u>Underline</u> any words you don't know, but don't worry about their meaning. How many words did you skip?

Write the words you underlined here:

Unknown word	Line number	Unknown word	Line number

Help Me Train My Pet

Dear Cat Whisperer,

My cat, Shadow, is always being naughty. At dinner time, he always jumps up on the table and tries to eat my food! When I put him on the floor he just jumps up again.
5 If I put him in the other room he meows loudly. My dog learned to follow the rules so quickly! Why isn't Shadow learning? Why is he so naughty? Can you give me some training tips?

Joan

Hi, Joan,

The first thing to remember is that cats and dogs think differently.

Next time you are preparing dinner, get Shadow's food ready, too. Before you sit down to eat, put Shadow in another room with his food dish. This way he won't come to you
5 when you are having dinner.

When training Shadow, be strict but don't get angry. Cats get scared easily. If he's scared, he will not want to learn rules in the future.

However, when Shadow does something good, always
10 praise him. Pet him and say, "Good!" or give him a treat. This tells him that you are happy.

Don't always respond when Shadow meows from the other room. Sometimes he just wants your attention. If Shadow learns that you will come any time he calls, he will
15 meow all the time!

The Cat Whisperer

216 words   **Time taken** _____

Reading Comprehension

Choose the correct answers. Try to answer the questions without looking up the meaning of the unknown word(s) in a dictionary.

1 What is Joan's problem?
   a She breaks the rules.
   b She can't train her dog.
   c She jumps on the dinner table.
   d She can't train her cat.

2 What tip did the Cat Whisperer give Joan?
   a Spend more time with Shadow.
   b Do not get angry at Shadow.
   c Feed Shadow after the people in the house.
   d Always respond when Shadow meows.

3 According to the Cat Whisperer, which of these statements about cats is true?
   a They think the same as dogs.
   b The get scared easily.
   c They like to be left alone.
   d They only meow when they are hungry.

4 How should Joan praise the cat?
   a She should come when he calls.
   b She should dance and sing.
   c She should say something positive.
   d She should pick the animal up.

5 Shadow will meow all the time if Joan _____ .
   a puts his food in another room
   b responds every time he meows
   c pets Shadow more than she pets the dog
   d scares him when she is training him

SELF CHECK

Write a short answer to each of the following questions.

1 Look again at the vocabulary learning tips on pages 6–7. Which of these tips do you think is most useful? Why?

_____

_____

2 What do you usually do when you find a word you don't know?

_____

_____

3 Do you think that you can still understand a passage if you skip some unknown words? Why or why not?

_____

_____

4 Which of the six reading passages in units 7–9 did you enjoy most? Why?

_____

_____

5 Which of the six reading passages in units 7–9 was easiest? Which was most difficult? Why?

Easiest: _____

Most difficult: _____

Why? _____

6 What have you read in English outside of class recently?

_____

_____

7 Are you keeping a vocabulary notebook?

_____

8 How will you try to improve your reading fluency from now on?

_____

_____

Fluency Practice

Time yourself as you read through the passage. Try to read as fluently as you can. Record your time in the Reading Rate Chart on page 176. Then answer the questions on the next page.

Running the Distance

Running a hundred kilometers a day is normal for Scott Jurek. He's one of the most successful long-distance runners in the world.
5 He often competes in races and breaks records. In 2010, Jurek set an American record by running 266.6 kilometers in one day. During the race, he ate while running and only stopped
10 to use the bathroom.

Jurek runs in what are called ultramarathons. An ultramarathon is any race that is longer than a marathon (42.2 km). Ultramarathons can take
15 place anywhere, and many races are held in places like deserts and mountain areas. Many of these races go on for days. The longest official ultramarathon is The Ultimate Ultra, in New York. It is 1,300 miles (2,000 km) long, and participants have to run more than 110 kilometers
20 a day. However, another event, the Trans America Footrace, goes from Los Angeles to New York—over 5,000 kilometers!

To give his body enough energy to run such long distances, Jurek is very careful about what he eats. He's vegan, so he doesn't eat meat, dairy, or eggs. He starts his day with a smoothie made of ingredients like almonds, bananas, salt, vanilla, and dried coconut. For
25 lunch and dinner he eats huge salads, sweet potatoes, and beans.

Of course, running ultramarathons is challenging for Jurek's body. But he believes that ultrarunning is actually more difficult for the mind than it is for the body.

233 words   **Time taken** _____

Reading Comprehension

Choose the correct answers.

1 What happened in 2010?
   a Jurek ran his first ultramarathon.
   b Jurek ran longer in one day than anyone ever before in America.
   c Jurek started training to run ultramarathons.
   d Jurek moved to America.

2 What is an ultramarathon?
   a a race that is longer than a marathon
   b a short race run by at least 1,000 people
   c a race that takes longer than ten days to run
   d a person who has run in at least 100 races

3 What does Jurek eat?
   a only meat
   b a mix of meat, eggs, and fruit
   c a lot of fruit, nuts, and vegetables
   d salads and a lot of pasta

4 According to the passage, what does Jurek do so he can run long distances?
   a He goes swimming every day.
   b He is careful about what he eats.
   c He eats a lot of meat and eggs.
   d He runs 110 km every day.

5 What does Jurek think is most challenging about ultrarunning?
   a dealing with your thoughts
   b caring about your feet
   c breathing easily
   d not getting sick when running

Review Reading 6: At the Movies: Bollywood

At the Movies: Bollywood

Bollywood is the largest movie-making business in India—and the world. In recent years, Bollywood films have become popular around the world.

What is Bollywood?

The word *Bollywood* is a mix of the words *Bombay* (a city in India now called
5 Mumbai) and *Hollywood*. Every year, Bollywood makes more movies and money than Hollywood does.

What are Bollywood movies like?

Certain features make Bollywood films different.
First, most Bollywood films are a minimum of three
10 hours long. The movie usually stops in the middle
and people take a short break.

Another important part of Bollywood movies is
music. Singing and dancing is very common
in Bollywood films. The music is often a mix
15 of Hindi pop songs and traditional melodies.
Some people think the music is as important
as the story. In some Indian theaters, people
watching the movie will sing and dance with the
performers on screen!

20 Bollywood's Popularity

For many decades, Bollywood films were only popular in India. But today
Bollywood movies are becoming popular around the world. Some Hollywood
movies are now copying Bollywood styles. In addition, some famous
Bollywood actors are now working in Hollywood films.

189 words   **Time taken** _____

Reading Comprehension

Choose the correct answers.

1 Why is the movie industry in India called *Bollywood*?
   a It was started in Hollywood.
   b The first Bollywood actor was named Bolly.
   c It's the Hollywood of Bombay (Mumbai).
   d It means *singing and dancing* in Hindi.

2 What does the passage say is a feature of Bollywood films?
   a fighting and car chases
   b love and marriage
   c singing and dancing
   d all of the above

3 Which is NOT true about Bollywood?
   a It is the largest movie-making industry in India.
   b It remakes Hollywood movies using Indian actors.
   c It is popular all around the world.
   d It makes more money than Hollywood.

4 According to the passage, what do some people do when they watch Bollywood movies?
   a They are very quiet during the show.
   b They talk on their cell phones.
   c They sing and dance with the people on the screen.
   d They throw trash at the movie screen.

5 According to the passage, what is happening now?
   a Some Hollywood films are copying Bollywood.
   b Famous Hollywood actors are working in Bollywood.
   c People are downloading Bollywood movies on the Internet.
   d all of the above

Fashion and Trends

Getting Ready

Discuss these questions with a partner.

1   Look at the people's clothes in the pictures above. What are they wearing?
2   What are you wearing now? What colors are your clothes?
3   What clothing styles are popular now? Do you like them? Why?

CHAPTER 1 Fashion Focus: Street Style

Before You Read
Fashion on the Street

A **Look quickly at the passage on the next page. Think about answers to these questions.**

   1 The people in the passage had their photos taken while they were walking down the street. Why would someone want to take their photos?
   2 What do you think *street style* is?
      a a place beautiful people go
      b a new way of finding fashion
      c a new kind of clothing

B **Discuss your answers with a partner.**

Reading Skill
Understanding Main Ideas in Paragraphs

> The *main idea* of a paragraph is the most important point. Usually, the first or second sentence in a paragraph gives the main idea. By understanding the main idea of each paragraph, you can also understand the main idea of the whole passage.

A **Read each pair of sentences below. Then read the passage on the next page. Which sentence is the main idea of each paragraph? Check (✓) your answer.**

Paragraph 1

☐ **a** Paris and New York are fashionable cities.
☐ **b** Fashion is important to people around the world.

Paragraph 2

☐ **a** Bloggers write about street fashion in many cities.
☐ **b** Scott Schuman started a fashion blog.

Paragraph 3

☐ **a** Bloggers use the Internet to show what is cool right now.
☐ **b** Bloggers can put photos online in a few minutes.

Paragraph 4

☐ **a** Small cities have street fashion blogs.
☐ **b** Your city could have a street fashion blog.

B **What is *street style*? Which paragraph(s) on the next page say what *street style* means?**

C **Read the passage on the next page again. Then answer the questions on page 128.**

> **Set a class goal for reading rate and comprehension.** Before you begin reading, set a class goal for reading fluency. What do you want your class average for words-per-minute to be for this reading? Having class goals to work towards can help you become a better reader.

Focus on Street Style

1 "People **dress** differently in New York and Paris," says Scott Schuman, who writes a blog about **fashion**. People in cities around the world **pay attention** to their clothes, and
5 they work hard to look beautiful. They use their culture and the materials around them to create their own look.

2 Schuman started his blog to "**simply** share photos of people that I saw on the streets
10 of New York." He thought the people looked fashionable, and he put photos online. Schuman isn't alone. Bloggers all around the world are using their cameras to **report** what is happening in their home cities. Since
15 bloggers find and write about stylish people on the street, this type of fashion is called *street* **style**.

Fashion changes often. With the Internet, street style changes even more quickly. Bloggers only need minutes to **snap a picture** and post it online. Their readers can use those ideas to create their own styles. Fashion used to come from the **runways** of Paris and Milan. Now fashion is homegrown.

Do you think your city is fashionable? Go online! There are street style blogs for most cities around the world, even small ones. Does your city have one?

3

20

4 25

Reading Comprehension
Check Your Understanding

A **Choose the correct answers.**

1 According to the passage, which statement is NOT true?
   a People work hard to create their own look.
   b Each city has its own identity.
   c People in Paris and New York dress the same.

2 Why did Scott Schuman start taking photos of street style?
   a He saw many fashionable people.
   b He worked for a fashion magazine.
   c He wanted to be more fashionable.

3 According to the passage, how do people use fashion blogs?
   a to say bad things about unfashionable people
   b to create their own styles
   c to learn about styles from the past

4 Where is street style happening?
   a mainly in New York and Paris
   b all around the world
   c on fashion show runways

B **Read the sentences below. In which paragraph (1–4) can you find the information? (Circle) the number.**

You want to know . . .	This information is in paragraph . . .			
1 how the Internet affects street style.	1	2	3	4
2 what Scott Schuman does.	1	2	3	4
3 which cities have street style blogs.	1	2	3	4

Critical Thinking

C **1** What do you think of street fashion? Is it interesting to you?
   2 Are there places in your city where you can see many fashionable people?
   3 Do you think people are too interested in fashion? Is what people wear important?

Vocabulary Comprehension
Words in Context

A **In each sentence, (circle) the best answer. The words in blue are from the passage.**

1 Your sister really has style. She wears _____ clothes.
   a great   b ugly

2 Those students never pay attention. They are always _____.
   a listening quietly   b talking and playing games

3 I like to dress simply. I _____ wear bright colors and jewelry.
   a love to   b rarely

4 The newspaper reported the accident. That's why I _____ all of the details.
   a know   b don't know

5   Fashion magazines usually tell you about the most popular _____.
    a   music   **b**   clothing
6   That man is snapping many pictures. He must be a _____.
    a   film maker   **b**   photographer
7   Please dress nicely for Saturday's party. You should wear _____.
    a   jeans and a T-shirt   **b**   your favorite suit or dress
8   I like to see models on the runway. They always look so beautiful _____.
    a   on the street   **b**   at fashion shows

B   **Answer the questions below. Discuss your answers with a partner.**

1   Is fashion important to you? Why?
    _____

2   Do you pay attention to new styles?
    _____

3   Who do you know who dresses well? Would someone want to snap a
    picture of them for their fashion blog?
    _____

A   **What nouns go with the verbs in the table below? Check (✓) the nouns that can go with each verb.**

	sunglasses	shoes	a jacket	a necktie	makeup	a dress
put on						
try on						
button						
tie						
zip up						
wear						

B   **Complete the chart with a verb with the opposite meaning.**

Verb		Opposite
1	put on	
2	get dressed	
3	tie	
4	button	
5	zip up	*unzip*

Vocabulary Skill
Verbs Used with Clothing

In this chapter, you learned the verbs *dress* and *pay attention*. In other units, you learned the verbs *wear*, *put on*, and *take off*. In English, there are many verbs used with clothing and other things relating to our appearance (*sunglasses, makeup,* etc.).

CHAPTER 2 From Trash to Fashion

Before You Read
Recycled Fashion Show

A Think about answers to these questions.

1 Look at the words below. Which of these things do you own?

> backpack   bicycle   cell phone
> keys   skirt   wallet

2 What do you do when these items are dirty or broken?
3 Look at the title of the passage on the next page. Look at the photo. What do you think the dress in the photo is made from?

B Discuss your answers with a partner.

Reading Skill
Reading for Details

When we read for details, we read slowly. For example, when we read instructions to understand how something works, we read carefully so we do not miss something important.

A Read the headlines of the passage on the next page. Read the sentences below. Write a check (✓) next to the sentences you predict will be true.

An Unusual City

☐ **a** People in Austin are very friendly and work hard.
☐ **b** People in Austin like to be strange and interesting.

Remember to Recycle

☐ **a** Austin has an art event every year to get people to recycle.
☐ **b** The people in Austin recycle more than people in any other city in the United States.

Recycling Can Be Creative

☐ **a** Wearing second-hand clothes is fun.
☐ **b** People can make these kind of clothes themselves.

B Carefully read the passage on the next page. Were your predictions in A correct?

C Read the passage again. Then answer the questions on page 132.

Recycled Fashion Show

What happens when fashionable people start **recycling**? A recycled-clothing fashion show, of course!

An Unusual City

5 The people of Austin, Texas, aren't afraid to **admit** they live in an interesting city. The city slogan is *Keep Austin **Weird***, and the city has many hip[1] cafés and stores. There are also a lot of people in Austin who work hard to **take care of** the
10 environment. Recycling and being eco-friendly is so important in Austin that the city is sometimes called America's greenest city.

Remember to Recycle

One of the most interesting ways that people help
15 the environment in Austin is by creating recycled fashion. Every year, the Austin Museum of Art has the *Keep Austin Beautiful Recycled Fashion Show*. They have the show to **remind** people to recycle.

More than 20 designers **come up with** clothes
20 from recycled materials for the show. In recent shows, **designers** have used plastic bags, old furniture, bike tires, and second-hand clothes.

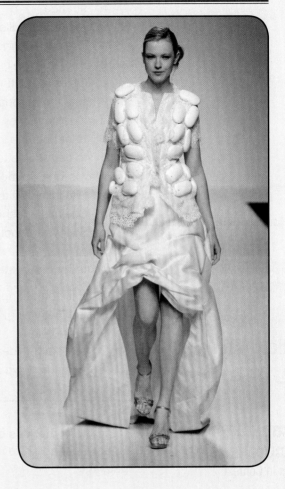

Recycling Can Be Creative

Recently, designer Tina Sparkles created a dress
25 **made out of** colorful computer wires[2] for the show. Later, Tina wrote a book about how to make recycled clothes called *Little Green Dresses*. Tina and the other designers in the Recycled Fashion Show believe that fashion is a great do-it-yourself (DIY) activity.

By creating their clothes from recycled materials, the designers are helping to keep Austin clean. They are also showing people that recycling can be a creative activity.

30 "I love fashion so much and I want to feel good about it," Tina says.

---

[1] Something that is **hip** is very cool or stylish.
[2] A **wire** is a long, thin piece of metal used to carry electricity.

Try it again! Try reading this passage again to see if you can read it more fluently. Reading this passage up to three times before answering the comprehension questions will help you improve your reading fluency.

Reading Comprehension
Check Your Understanding

A **Choose the correct answers.**

1 Which of the following does NOT describe Austin, Texas?
   a strange   **b** different   **c** boring

2 Why is Austin called America's greenest city?
   a The city has many trees and flowers.
   b People there care about the environment.
   c Cafés in Austin must recycle their trash.

3 What is the purpose of the fashion show?
   a to raise money for a recycling center
   b to get people interested in recycling
   c to get people to come to the art museum

4 Why is Tina Sparkles mentioned in the passage?
   a She invented the idea of recycled fashion.
   b She has a fashion blog about recycled fashion.
   c She wrote about about how to make recycled fashion.

B **Discuss these questions with a partner.**

1 What is something that you recycled recently?
2 Besides recycling, can you come up with other ways to be eco-friendly?

Critical Thinking

C **1** Do you like the idea of using recycled things for fashion?
   2 What things do you own that you could recycle into fashion?

Vocabulary Comprehension
Words in Context

A **Read the sentences below. Check (✓) true (T) or false (F). If the statement is false, change it to make it true. The words in blue are from the passage.**

		T	F
1	If you recycle something, then it becomes something new.		
2	A designer is a person who flies an airplane.		
3	To look after something is to take care of it.		
4	You can use a calendar to remind yourself about important meetings.		
5	A house made out of grass will be very strong.		
6	When you admit to doing something, you say you did it.		
7	To come up with an idea means to think of something new.		
8	If your friends are weird, they do very normal things in their free time.		

B Complete the sentences with words in blue from **A**. You might have to change the form of the words.

1 It's 3:30. Please _____ Mr. Jones that he has a meeting at 4:00.

2 Did you _____ an answer to my question?

3 This can is _____ aluminum. You can _____ it.

4 This painting looks very _____. Do you know what it is supposed to be?

A Complete the word web below with words from the box.

belt	bikini	blouse	boots	coat
dress	earrings	jacket	jeans	sandals
shirt	shorts	skirt	slippers	suit
sunglasses	sweater	T-shirt	tie	watch

Vocabulary Skill
Word Webs

When you link related words and ideas together, it is easier to remember them. A word web can help you organize and remember new vocabulary.

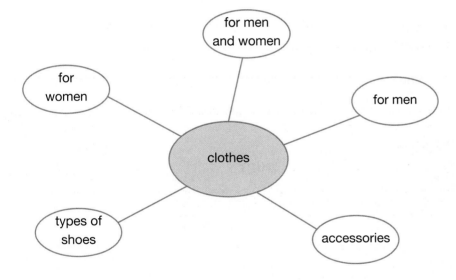

B What other words can you add to the word web? Share your ideas with a partner.

Real Life Skill
Understanding Clothing Labels

Clothing labels tell you how to clean and care for your clothes. When you read clothing labels, you often see certain words.

A Look at the list of fabrics (clothing material) in the box. Which ones do you know? Use your dictionary to help you understand the new words. Which fabrics do you wear in summer? In winter? All year round?

| cotton | fake fur | leather | linen | polyester | silk | wool |

B How do you clean clothes? Label each picture with a verb from the box.

dry
hand wash
hang dry
iron
machine wash

1. _____

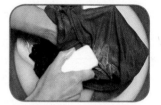

2. _____

3. _____

4. _____

5. _____

C Sentences 1–4 below are about the clothing labels shown here. Check (✓) true (T) or false (F).

JACKET
100% LINEN
HAND WASH IN COLD WATER
LAY FLAT TO DRY
MEDIUM TO HOT IRON

SHIRT
50% polyester / 50% cotton
Machine wash warm
Dry on low heat

DRESS
100% wool
HAND WASH ONLY

		T	F
1	It is best to wash all three items in warm water.		
2	You can wash the shirt and the jacket in a washing machine.		
3	You can dry only the dress in a dryer.		
4	You cannot iron any of the clothes.		

What do you think?

1 What is the most unusual fashion now for men? For women?
2 What clothes or accessories do you think look good on a woman? On a man?

A Mysterious World

Getting Ready

Discuss these questions with a partner.

1 Who usually solves mysteries?
2 What tools do you need to solve mysteries?
3 Have you ever solved a mystery? How did you solve it?

CHAPTER 1 A Mysterious Book

Before You Read
Writing in Code

A **Think about answers to these questions.**

1 Why do people use codes? What kinds of things do people write in code?
2 Have you and a friend ever had a secret code or language?

B **Discuss your answers with a partner.**

Reading Skill
Making and Checking
Predictions

When we read, we often predict (guess) what we will read next. For example, we use this skill when we are reading stories. As we read, we also check to see if our predictions were correct.

A **Read the title of the passage on the next page and the pictures. What do you think this book is about?**

_____

_____.

B **The book in the passage on the next page is written in code. Why do you think the writer used a code? Tell a partner.**

_____

_____.

C **Now read the passage on the next page. Then answer the questions on page 138.**

The World's Most Mysterious Manuscript[1]

In 1912, book dealer Wilfrid Voynich bought **a number of** books in Italy. He bought so many that he didn't look very closely at the books he was purchasing. When he got home, he

5 **discovered** he had bought a very strange **handwritten** manuscript. It was written in a language he had never seen before. It was also **full of** pictures of plants.

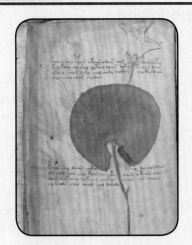

Since then, the book—now known as the

10 Voynich Manuscript—has become known as the world's most **mysterious** manuscript. It has been studied by many people, including professors, codebreakers, and language **experts**. However, no one has ever discovered

15 its meaning or **author**.

There are many ideas about who wrote it and why. Some people say that a famous scientist like Francis Bacon wrote it. Other people think it could be a religious text.[2] Some other people think the

20 manuscript is a great hoax and doesn't **mean** anything at all.

Scientists have learned that the manuscript was made between 1404 and 1438. However, this only tells us how old the paper is, not when the

25 book was written. But there's still hope that the manuscript is real and that there's meaning to its words.

The Voynich Manuscript remains a mystery today, but the pages are on the Internet if you would like

30 to try to crack the code.

---

[1] A **manuscript** is an unprinted book.
[2] A **religious text** is a book about a god or gods.

Reading Comprehension
Check Your Understanding

A **Choose the correct answers.**

1 Why is the manuscript mysterious?
  a No one knows if Wilfrid Voynich is real.
  b No one understands the manuscript.
  c No one can find the manuscript now.

2 What is in the manuscript?
  a pictures of plants
  b pictures about religion
  c pictures of famous scientists

3 When was the manuscript's paper probably made?
  a 1348
  b 1404
  c 1912

4 Why do we call it the Voynich Manuscript?
  a Wilfrid Voynich wrote it.
  b The author uses the word *Voynich* a lot.
  c It was found by Wilfrid Voynich.

B **Are these statements about the Voynich Manuscript true or false? Check (✓) true (T) or false (F).**

		T	F
1	Wilfrid Voynich bought the manuscript in China.		
2	The manuscript is written in a strange language.		
3	Many people today want to know what the manuscript means.		
4	Experts say that Wilfrid Voynich wrote the manuscript.		

Critical Thinking

C **1** Are mysteries like the Voynich Manuscript interesting to you? Why or why not?

2 Why might someone create a book in a language no one understands?

Learning new vocabulary can be fun. Learning new vocabulary can be one of the most enjoyable parts of becoming a good reader. In addition to the vocabulary that is explicitly taught in this chapter, are there other words related to the topic that you would like to learn?

Vocabulary Comprehension
Words in Context

A **In each sentence, (circle) the best answer. The words in blue are from the passage.**

1 If you discover something, you _____ it.
  a find   **b** look for

2 A mysterious person loves to _____ .
  a tell jokes   **b** keep secrets

3 Joe is a football expert! He _____!
   a has never played   **b** knows every rule

4 Stephenie Meyer is my favorite author. I have _____.
   a read all of her books   **b** watched all of her films

5 The word *friendly* means _____.
   a rude   **b** kind

6 Which of these is more likely to be handwritten?
   a a postcard   **b** a business letter

7 My science notebook _____, but my math notebook is full of notes.
   a is empty   **b** has writing on every page

8 If there are a number of activities for students to do after school, there are _____ activities.
   a many different   **b** one or two

B **Answer the questions below. Discuss your answers with a partner.**

   1 Would you rather send a handwritten letter or an email to your friends?
   2 Who is your favorite author? Is he or she an expert in anything?
   3 Would you rather be an expert in one subject or know a little about a number of subjects?

A **Read the sentences below. For each word, find an antonym from the passage.**

   1 well-understood *mysterious*   **4** truth _____
   2 lost _____   **5** empty _____
   3 few _____   **6** beginner _____

B **Complete the sentences below with an antonym from A. You might have to change the form of the word or phrase.**

   1 My coworkers told me I was going to be fired today, but it was only a _____.
   2 My brother is a marketing _____; he can sell anything.
   3 The bus was _____ children; no one else could get on.
   4 Do you think Christopher Columbus _____ America?
   5 Choose whichever shirt you like; we have _____ colors.
   6 A number of people say they have seen _____ lights in the sky over the desert.

Vocabulary Skill
Antonyms

In this chapter, you learned the words *serious* and *funny*. These words are *antonyms*: words with opposite meanings. By learning antonyms you can increase your vocabulary in English.

Before You Read
Sometimes Things
Disappear

A **Think about answers to these questions.**

1 Have you ever lost your cell phone or your keys? What is something you lost recently? Did you find it?

2 Do you know of any unsolved crimes? Do you think they can be easily solved?

B **Discuss your answers with a partner.**

Reading Skill
Skimming for the
Main Idea

You *skim* to get a general idea about a passage. When you skim, look quickly at the title and the photos. Then read the first and last sentences of each paragraph. You can use this general information to predict what a passage is about.

A **Skim the passage on the next page. Then complete the sentence below.**

This passage is about a man who _____ .
a won $200,000
b disappeared
c flew a plane to Mexico

B **Now read the entire passage slowly. Was your answer in A correct?**

C **Read the passage again. Then answer the questions on page 142.**

A sense of personal satisfaction. One of the greatest rewards of reading is the personal satisfaction you get as you see the improvements you make. Pause now and think about ways that your enjoyment of reading has changed over the past few weeks.

Into the Night Sky

On November 24, 1971, a very **curious** thing happened. A man using the name Dan Cooper bought
5 a plane ticket for a short **flight** across the state of Washington. Nobody knew it at the time, but Dan Cooper was not his real
10 name.

After the plane took off, Cooper told a flight attendant that he was carrying a bomb.[1] He **demanded**
15 $200,000 and parachutes.[2] The pilot[3] sent a message to the airport, and they called the police. When the plane landed, Cooper allowed all of the **passengers** to get off safely. Once the money and parachutes were delivered, the plane **took off** again.

Only the pilot, copilot, and one flight attendant were on the plane with Cooper.
20 He told the pilot to fly to Mexico City. He **gave instructions** to fly low to the ground and slowly.

Cooper then put the whole crew in the cockpit[4] at the front of the plane. He tied the money to his body. He opened a door at the back of the plane. The night was cold, rainy, and pitch black.[5] It must not have **worried** him, as he
25 jumped into the darkness.

No one ever saw Cooper or the money again. The police have talked to hundreds of people about the **case**, but it is still unsolved.

[1] A **bomb** is a dangerous weapon that explodes.
[2] A **parachute** is something that lets a person jump from an airplane and float safely to the ground.
[3] A **pilot** is a person who flies an airplane.
[4] The **cockpit** is the place in a plane where the pilot sits.
[5] If a place is **pitch black**, it is completely dark.

Reading Comprehension
Check Your Understanding

A Choose the correct answers.

1 Why did Cooper demand parachutes?
  a He was afraid of flying.
  b He planned to jump out of the plane.
  c He planned to make the passengers jump out of the plane.

2 What did Cooper tell the pilot to do?
  a jump out of the plane
  b fly the plane to Mexico City
  c crash the plane after he jumped

3 Where did the money come from?
  a Cooper stole the money from a bank.
  b The police gave it to Cooper.
  c Cooper found it on the airplane.

4 Cooper _____.
  a was scared of the dark
  b worked for the police
  c has not been found

B Read the sentences below. Check (✔) true (T) or false (F). If the statement is false, change it to make it true.

		T	F
1	Cooper bought a train ticket.		
2	Cooper took the parachute onto the plane with him.		
3	The police know what Cooper's real name is.		

Critical Thinking

C 1 What do you think about Cooper's plan? Why do you think he has never been found?

2 Could someone do this today? Why or why not?

Vocabulary Comprehension
Odd Word Out

A For each group of words, circle the word that does not belong. The words in blue are from the passage.

1	flight	airplane	crew
2	demand	do	tell
3	flight attendant	pilot	passenger
4	tell what to do	give instructions	tell a secret
5	take off	fly	watch
6	scared	happy	worried
7	solution	case	project
8	curious	strange	normal

B Complete the sentences with words in blue from **A**. You might have to change the form of the words.

1 The teacher _____ to the students before handing out the assignment.
2 I would like to buy a ticket for the next _____ to Sydney.
3 The police officers were busy because they had a lot of _____ to solve.
4 I was alone on the bus. There were no other _____ except for me.

A Read the words below. Use a dictionary to understand each word's meaning. Which of the words down the left can make phrases with the words along the top? Check all (✔) the words that go together.

Vocabulary Skill
Travel

In the passage, you read the words *ticket*, *flight*, *plane*, and *airport*. Each of these is quite general, and you can add adjectives to each word to make them more specific.

	ticket	flight	plane	airport
round-trip	✔			
domestic				
private				
commercial				
non-refundable				
direct				
passenger				
international				

B Complete each sentence below with a phrase from the box. You might have to change the form of the word.

1 If you take a(n) _____ to New York from Japan, you won't have to change planes in San Francisco.
2 The company has a(n) _____ for its managers to use.
3 The flight from Paris to Beijing leaves from a(n) _____ airport.
4 Sarah bought a(n) _____ for her trip to Berlin and back.
5 I'm sorry. You bought a(n) _____ , so I can't give your money back.
6 You don't need your passport if you take a(n) _____ .
7 The 737 is the world's most popular _____ . People all around the world have been using it since 1965.
8 To fly from one city to another in the same country, you need to go to a(n) _____ .

Real Life Skill

Dictionary Skills: Choosing the Right Definition

> Many words in English have more than one definition. Your dictionary can help you understand different meanings of the same word.

A The words below have more than one definition. Complete sentences 1–6 below with the correct words. You might have to change the form of the words. Use the dictionary definitions to help you.

dead *adj.* **1** not alive; **2** quiet, boring
curious *adj.* **1** wanting to know more; **2** very strange or unusual
rate 1 *n.* price, the cost of something; **2** *v.* to say how good something is
notice 1 *n.* a piece of paper saying something important; **2** *v.* to see something small and important
kid 1 *n.* a young child (informal); **2** *v.* to say something in a funny or joking way
serious *adj.* **1** quiet, humorless; **2** very bad

		Definition	
		1	**2**
1	This milk has a _____ taste. Is it old?		
2	This nightclub is _____! There are only two people here.		
3	The plane ticket is usually $1,500, but I bought it online and got a cheaper _____.		
4	Alex is usually so _____, but today he told a very funny joke in class.		
5	There is a stain on my shirt. I didn't _____ it until just now.		
6	Ms. Williams has 25 _____ in her first-grade class.		

B For each sentence in A, which definition (1 or 2) did you use? Check (✔) your answers.

What do you think?

1 Are you interested in mysteries? What is your favorite mystery?
2 Have you ever seen anything mysterious, or has something mysterious ever happened to you? What happened?

Getting Ready

Discuss these questions with a partner.

1 Look at the photos above. Where do you get your news from?

2 Why do you get your news from that source? Which source above do you think is most interesting? Which is most useful?

CHAPTER 1 Face to Face with a Chupacabra

Before You Read
Stories about Vampires

A **Think about answers to these questions.**

1 The story on the next page is about a *vampire*. What does a vampire do? Complete the sentence below.

A vampire . . .
a drinks your blood.
b gives you wishes.
c takes your money.

2 Look at the picture on the next page and the title of the passage. Have you ever heard of a chupacabra? What do you think it does?

B **Discuss your answers with a partner.**

Reading Skill
Understanding the Order of Events

> In passages about an order of events, you often see words and phrases about time: *at first, then, suddenly, that's when.* You can also look for other clues. A person's name or a noun is usually given first, then followed in later sentences by pronouns like *he, she, it,* and *we.*

A **The sentences below are from the passage on the next page. Put the events in the correct order from 1–6.**

_1_ **a** My mother and I were watching a movie.
____ **b** My mother and I went outside to find out what the noise was.
____ **c** Suddenly, we heard a loud noise in the yard.
____ **d** I thought it was a large dog at first.
____ **e** That's when we saw this . . . thing.
____ **f** But then it stood up on two legs—like a man!

B **Now read lines 8–16 in the passage on the next page. Were your answers in A correct?**

C **Read the rest of the interview. Then answer the questions on page 148.**

> **Evaluate your progress.** In what ways are you better today than you were earlier in this reading course? What things do you still need to work on to become a better reader? When you read the review units, use the reading rate and reading comprehension charts at the end of the book to evaluate your progress as a reader.

www.truestories.heinle.com/chupacabra

Face to Face with a Chupacabra: An Interview

For years, people in North and South America have told stories about the **chupacabra**. *Chupacabra* is Spanish for *goat sucker*. In this issue, Maria Teresa

5 Perez, 24, from Chile, tells us her story.

Mystery Magazine: Tell us about that night. What happened?

Maria: My mother and I were watching a movie. It was late—maybe midnight.

10 Suddenly,[1] we heard a loud **noise** in the yard.[2] We have chickens and other animals there. My mother and I went outside to **find out** what the noise was. That's when we saw this . . . thing. I thought it was a large dog at first. It was dark,

15 so I couldn't see well. But then it **stood up** on two legs—like a man! It was over a meter tall with red eyes and large teeth.

Mystery Magazine: What did you do?

Maria: My mom and I **screamed**, and the thing **ran away**. Or maybe it flew. It moved as fast as a bird.

20 **Mystery Magazine:** What happened to the animals?

Maria: Five chickens were dead. But the chupacabra didn't eat them. It drank their blood.

Mystery Magazine: So do you **believe** it was a chupacabra?

Maria: It was like a **nightmare**—a really scary dream—but I know it was **real**. Many

25 people in Chile, Brazil, Mexico, even the U.S. have seen this thing. I hope I never see it again.

---

[1] If something happens **suddenly**, it happens quickly and without warning.
[2] A **yard** is an open area next to a house for plants and animals.

Face to Face with a Chupacabra   147

Reading Comprehension
Check Your Understanding

A Choose the correct answers.

1 Where have people seen the chupacabra?
   a only North America
   b only South America
   c both North and South America

2 Which of these statements about the chupacabra is correct?
   a It looks like a large dog.
   b It stands on two legs.
   c It is two meters tall.

3 How does Maria feel about the chupacabra?
   a She's angry because it killed her chickens.
   b She's afraid of it.
   c She thinks it's funny.

4 Does Maria think she saw a chupacabra?
   a Yes, she does.
   b No, she thinks it was a bad dream.
   c Maybe. She doesn't know.

B Read the sentences about the chupacabra. Check (✓) true (T) or false (F). If the statement is false, change it to make it true.

		T	F
1	The chupacabra has red eyes and big teeth.		
2	The chupacabra was in the house.		
3	The chupacabra ate the chickens.		

Critical Thinking

C 1 Do you think Maria's story is true? Why?
   2 Does your country have stories about something like the chupacabra?

Vocabulary Comprehension
Words in Context

A In each sentence, (circle) the best answer. The words in blue are from the passage.

1 There is a lot of traffic noise in the _____.
   a countryside   b city

2 If you find out when the train is leaving, you _____ when it is leaving.
   a don't know   b learn

3 When the president entered the room, everyone _____.
   a stood up   b sat down

4 The little girl screamed "Help!" when she saw the _____.
   a cute little cat   b large dog

5 My dog ran away from home. I don't know why he _____.
   a left   b returned

6 Mary says her uncle is a famous actor, and I believe her. I _____ her story is true.

    a don't think   **b** think

7 Last night, I had a nightmare. It was a very _____ dream.

    a funny   **b** scary

8 A _____ is a real animal.

    a dragon   **b** horse

B **Answer the questions below. Discuss your answers with a partner.**

1 Do you believe ghosts are real? Why?

_____

2 Do you ever have nightmares? What happens in these dreams?

_____

3 Is there a lot of noise where you live?

_____

A **Read the sentences below. Use the words in blue to complete the chart.**

1 The building was on fire. On the eighth floor, a woman screamed, "Help!"

2 "Shhhhhh. We're in the library," whispered the teacher. "If you want to talk, speak softly."

3 Paco is in the living room. His sister is in the kitchen. "Hey, Maria! Can you bring me some water?" calls Paco.

4 "Yukiko, are you OK?" asks Simon.
"No," sighs Yukiko sadly. "My boyfriend and I had a fight."

5 Jan and Peter are at a noisy rock concert. Jan yells something to Peter. "What?" Peter shouts. "I can't hear you!"

Vocabulary Skill
Ways of Saying Things

In this chapter, you learned the verb *scream*. People make this sound when they are afraid or angry. A person can also scream words (for example, *No!*). There are many verbs in English that describe how people say things.

Words that describe loud sounds	Words that describe soft/quiet sounds
scream	

B **Read the sentences in A aloud.**

C **Write a short conversation of two to four sentences. Use words from the chart in A to show how the speakers are talking. Then practice your dialog with a partner.**

CHAPTER 2 Alive to Tell Their Tale

Before You Read
An Accident

A Look at the title of the passage on the next page and at the photos. What do you predict this passage is about? Complete the sentence:

1 Maybe this passage is about some men who _____.
   a tell stories about accidents
   b were trapped underground
   c live in a very strange place

2 Look at the pictures on the next page. What do the pictures tell you about the story?

B Discuss your answers with a partner.

Reading Skill
Making and Checking Predictions

> When you read, you can often predict what will come next. While you read, you also check to see if your predictions were correct. Good readers learn to make and check their predictions.

A Read paragraph 1 in the passage on the next page. Then stop and answer the questions below.

1 On August 5th, what happened to the 33 men? _____

2 Why were the men underground? _____

3 What do you think will happen next? _____

B Now read paragraph 2 in the passage on the next page. Then stop and answer the questions below.

1 Was your prediction in **A** correct? ☐ Yes ☐ No
2 How did rescue workers know the miners were alive? _____

3 What do you predict will happen next? _____

C Now read paragraph 3 in the passage on the next page. Then stop and answer the questions below.

1 Was your prediction in **B** correct? ☐ Yes ☐ No
2 How do you think this story ends? _____

D Now read the last paragraphs of the passage. Were your predictions correct? Read the whole passage again. Then answer the questions on page 152.

Alive to Tell Their Tale![1]

1 On August 5, 2010, an accident **trapped** 33 men 700 meters underground. The men worked for a copper and gold mine near Copiapó, Chile. At first, no one knew if the
5 miners had lived through the **accident**.

2 Then, on the morning of August 22, **rescue** workers made a hole deep enough to reach the miners. The men wrote notes and sent them up. The miners had **survived** by eating only
10 small bits of food at a time and drinking a little milk once a day. (The mine kept some food and drinks underground in case of an emergency.) They had used their **tools** to dig for water. They had used the batteries from machines to keep some lights on.

3 Once the miners were found, the rescue workers passed them food, water, books, and letters from their families. Even though the miners had been
15 found, the rescuers had to work hard to get them out. The rescuers needed a powerful drill to dig deep into the ground. It took 52 more days to save the men.

4 20 On the night of October 12, the workers were able to save the men. One by one the miners were brought up in a specially built **elevator**. They were weak, so the workers were very careful. Family members,
25 friends, and people around the world cheered and **celebrated**. Church bells rang throughout Chile.

5 In all, the miners spent 69 **terrifying** days underground.

"We had strength, . . . we wanted to fight for our families, and that was the greatest thing." said Luis Urzua, the
30 supervisor.[2] He was the last miner to be saved.

---

[1] A **tale** is a story.
[2] A **supervisor** is a manager or group leader who makes sure workers are working correctly.

Reading Comprehension
Check Your Understanding

A Choose the correct answers.

1 Where were the men trapped?
 a in an elevator
 b in a mine
 c in their office

2 Which of these does the passage NOT say the men did to survive?
 a dug for water
 b drank milk
 c made a fire

3 How were the men brought out of the mine?
 a in a special elevator
 b they climbed up a wide tunnel
 c by a very long ladder

4 How many days did the men spend in the mine?
 a 22
 b 52
 c 69

B Put the events of the Chilean miners' story in order from 1 to 7. Then retell their story to a partner.

_1_ a An accident trapped the miners.
____ b The men were brought out of the mine.
____ c The workers received letters from their families.
____ d The miners sent rescue workers a note asking for help.
____ e The workers dug for 52 days to save the miners.
____ f Rescue workers reached the miners.
____ g Rescue workers put the special elevator in the mine.

Critical Thinking

C 1 What do you think was the scariest part of the miners' story?
 2 What do you think the miners did first when they got home?

Vocabulary Comprehension
Words in Context

A In each sentence, (circle) the best answer. The words in blue are from the passage.

1 I usually take the elevator to my office on the _____ floor.
 a first   b ninth

2 Tommy didn't mean to _____. It was an accident.
 a break the window   b fix the window

3 You will need some tools if you are going to _____.
 a build a table   b eat dinner

4 Polar bears survive the winter in Antarctica by _____.
 a playing in the snow   b eating fish

5 Which of these can people trap?

    a mice   **b** fruit

6 At the pool, the lifeguard's job is to rescue people who _____.

    a can't swim   **b** break the rules

7 Which of these are you more likely to celebrate?

    a a birthday   **b** an exam

8 Which of these is more terrifying?

    a a sandwich   **b** an earthquake

B **Complete the sentences with the words in blue from A.**

1 The cat was meowing loudly when he got ___*trapped*___ in the box.

2 The taxi driver got into a(n) _____ because he was talking on his phone.

3 I don't like to walk up stairs. I want to take the _____.

4 You got an A+ on your test! Let's go out for dinner to _____.

A **Add the suffix -*ful* to the nouns in the box to form an adjective. Then match the new word with its definition.**

| color | help | joy | pain | play | youth |

Adjective	Definition
1 *colorful*	with a lot of color
2	kind, always helping
3	young
4	happy
5	hurting
6	not serious, funny

B **Complete the sentences below using the words from A.**

1 Bill has a toothache, and it's very _____.

2 The people in Pilobolus wear _____ costumes of blue, red, purple, and yellow.

3 Annette is a very _____ girl. She's always taking care of others.

4 My grandmother is 80 years old, but she still has a very _____ way of thinking.

Vocabulary Skill
The Suffix -*ful*

In this chapter, you read the word *careful*. The suffix -*ful* means *full of* (*care* + *ful* = full of care, to do something with a lot of care). There are many adjectives in English that end with the suffix -*ful*.

Why is reading important to you? Do you like to read? Why or why not? Remember that becoming a good reader will help you in many aspects of life, not just in this class. As you become a better reader you will be able to contribute more to your education and to your community.

Real Life Skill
Identifying Types of Books

In bookstores, books are grouped together by type. For example, books about countries and vacations are usually in the *travel section* of a bookstore. Knowing a book's type can help you find it faster.

A Match each type of book with its description.

1	romance	_____	**a**	scary stories
2	horror	_____	**b**	stories about real people and events
3	science fiction	_____	**c**	stories about the future, travel in space, etc.
4	mystery/thriller	_____	**d**	love stories
5	nonfiction	_____	**e**	an important work of writing
6	literature	_____	**f**	a story where you try to guess the ending

B Read the book titles and descriptions. What type of book is each one? Write the number from **A** in the chart. Some books are more than one type.

Book	Type of Book
The Time Machine *H. G. Wells* A man creates a machine and travels to the future. This book is read in many high school English classes.	3, 6
Angela's Ashes *Frank McCourt* The true story of a boy who grew up poor in Ireland. The story won a number of prizes.	
The Diary of a Young Girl *Anne Frank* The diary Anne Frank kept while hiding from the Nazis in the 1940s	
The Da Vinci Code *Dan Brown* A Frenchwoman and an American man try to find a killer. They fall in love during the adventure.	
Twilight *Stephenie Meyer* A story about a human girl who falls in love with a vampire boy.	
Life of Pi *Yann Martel* A young boy goes from India to North America by ship. The ship sinks, and the boy must share a small boat with a tiger. This book won a writing prize in 2002.	

What do you think?

1 Which story in this unit was more interesting to you? Why?

2 Both stories in this unit were about scary events. Do you know any scary stories? Tell the story to your partner.

In order to become a more fluent reader, remember to follow the six points of the ACTIVE approach—before, while, and after you read. See the inside front cover for more information on the ACTIVE approach.

Activate Prior Knowledge

Before you read, it's important to think about what you already know about the topic, and what you want to get from the text.

A **Look at the passage on the next page. Read only the title and look at the picture. What do you think the article is about?**

B **Now read the first paragraph of the passage. What do you know about the topic? What do you think the term *style rookie* means? Discuss with a partner.**

Cultivate Vocabulary

As you read, you may find words you do not know. Remember you do not need to understand all the words in a passage to understand it. Skip the unknown words for now, or guess what they mean. Underline new vocabulary. Write the new vocabulary in your vocabulary notebook. (See pages 6 and 7 for more advice on vocabulary.)

A **Now read the second paragraph. Underline any words or phrases you do not know. Can you understand the passage even if you do not understand all of the words?**

B **Write the unknown words here. Without using a dictionary, try to guess their meaning. Use the words around the unknown word to help you.**

New word/phrase	I think it means:

Think About Meaning

As you read, think about what you can infer, or guess about the author's intention, attitudes, and purpose for writing.

Read paragraphs 1 and 2 again. Discuss these questions with a partner.

- Who is Tavi Gevinson?
- How does the writer feel about Tavi Gevinson?
- Do you agree that a young person can understand fashion very well?

Increase Reading Fluency

To increase your reading fluency, it's important to monitor your own reading habits as you read. Look again at the tips on page 8. As you read, follow these tips.

Now read the whole passage *Style Rookie*. As you read, think about what you are learning.

Style Rookie

1 Tavi Gevinson is not like most high school girls. She picks out her own clothes and doesn't dress like the other girls at school. Tavi has many of her own
5 ideas about fashion, and she expresses them on her blog, *Style Rookie*. She often posts pictures from fashion shows and her own daily outfits.[1]

2 Tavi started her blog when she was in
10 middle school. Her fashion choices and opinions were very good. At first, many people thought a professional wrote it. Her blog got popular very quickly. After only eight months of writing *Style*
15 *Rookie*, Tavi started to get messages from some of her favorite designers.

3 Tavi's mother is an artist and her father is an English teacher. They didn't know about the blog until *The New York Times* asked to do an interview.[2] Now, Tavi's
20 father goes with her to fashion events around the world.

4 Since she appeared in the newspaper, Tavi's fame has grown. In 2010, Tavi designed her own T-shirt with a fashion company. She's also written stories for fashion magazines. In that same year she was the guest of famous designers at fashion events in New York, Paris, and Japan.

5 25 People all around the fashion world now take Tavi seriously. What does Tavi want to do when she grows up? She's already doing it!

218 words　　　**Time taken** _____

[1] An **outfit** is a set of clothing.
[2] An **interview** is when someone asks another person questions to find out about them.

Verify Strategies

To build your reading fluency, think about how you use strategies to read, and how successfully you are using them. Use the questions in the **Self Check** on the next page to think about your use of reading strategies.

Evaluate Progress

Evaluating your progress means thinking about how much you understood from the passage. Also, think about how fluently you were able to read the passage to get the information you needed.

Reading Comprehension

Choose the correct answers.

1 What is this passage about?
   a   fashion at American high schools
   b   a girl who learned about fashion in school
   c   a high school student with a fashion blog
   d   a high school that teaches fashion

2 How is Tavi different from other high school girls?
   a   She dresses differently.
   b   She has her own ideas about fashion.
   c   She writes the blog *Style Rookie*.
   d   She is interested in clothes.

3 Why did designers contact Tavi?
   a   They wanted to be like her.
   b   They liked her blog.
   c   They wanted to work for her.
   d   They wanted to meet Tavi's parents.

4 According to the passage, which newspaper did Tavi do an interview for?
   a   *Style Rookie*
   b   *Vogue*
   c   *The New York Times*
   d   her high school newspaper

5 Which is NOT true about Tavi?
   a   She has written articles for fashion magazines.
   b   She was a special guest at a few fashion shows.
   c   Her mother is an artist and her father is a teacher.
   d   She wants to be a flight attendant when she grows up.

SELF CHECK

A Here is a list of all the reading skills in *Active Skills for Reading, Intro.* For each skill, say whether you found the skill useful, not useful, or if you need more work with it. Check (✔) the correct boxes.

Reading skill	Useful	Not useful	Needs work
Identifying Similarities and Differences			
Making and Checking Predictions			
Making Inferences			
Predicting from the Title			
Reading for Details			
Recognizing Purpose			
Scanning			
Skimming			
Skimming for the Main Idea			
Understanding Cause and Effect			
Understanding Main Ideas			
Understanding Main Ideas in Paragraphs			
Understanding the Order of Events			

B Here are the four fluency strategies covered in the Review Units. For each strategy, say whether you found the strategy useful, not useful, or if you need more work with it. Check (✔) the correct boxes.

Reading skill	Useful	Not useful	Needs work
PRO			
SQ3R			
Dealing with Unknown Words			
Reading ACTIVEly			

C Look again at the *Are You an Active Reader?* quiz on page 10 and complete your answers again. How has your reading fluency improved since you started this course?

Celebrity Chef Anthony Bourdain

Anthony Bourdain is a celebrity chef, author, and television host. He has experience working as a chef in some of New York City's most
5 popular restaurants. He wrote a book about his adventures.[1]

The book became a favorite for food lovers. It tells stories about the way chefs really cook. Readers
10 learned that most kitchens are not sparkling clean and that many chefs are not trained.

Today, Bourdain is the host of a travel show about food. On the show, he travels to different cities learning about the local food and culture. He is very interested in the
15 relationships people have with their food.

On the show, Bourdain has traveled to dozens[2] of places. He hunted and ate lizards[3] in Saudi Arabia. He helped make kimchi in Korea. He explored bat caves in Jamaica. He has also filmed his show in places like Ghana and Tahiti.

Bourdain has said that he loves eating Vietnamese food and that he wants to live in
20 Vietnam someday. It is his favorite country. But for now, he will continue to host his show and work as a chef at his famous New York City restaurant.

191 words   Time taken _____

[1] An **adventure** is an unusual, exciting, or dangerous trip.
[2] If you have a **dozen** things, you have 12 of them.

[3] a **lizard**.

Reading Comprehension

Choose the correct answers.

1 How did Anthony Bourdain become a famous chef?
   a He used to host a television show.
   b He traveled to different cities.
   c He has eaten unusual foods.
   d He wrote a book about cooking.

2 Why was Bourdain's first book popular?
   a It explained how to cook.
   b It told secrets about the restaurant business.
   c It was full of interesting travel stories.
   d It talked about unusual foods from around the world.

3 What does Bourdain NOT do on his television show?
   a travel to unusual places
   b start new restaurants
   c learn about cooking
   d talk to people about food

4 Why does Bourdain travel the world?
   a He wants to be a famous explorer.
   b He wants new ideas for his restaurant.
   c He likes talking to people about food.
   d He wants to teach people how to eat healthier.

5 Why does Bourdain want to live in Vietnam?
   a He has many friends there.
   b He wants to learn Vietnamese.
   c He used to work in a restaurant there.
   d He likes the country a lot.

Review Reading 8: Just A Dream?

Just a Dream?

Adrian Hayward is a big soccer fan. In 2005, he had a strange dream. In the dream, Hayward was watching a soccer game. He saw Xabi Alonso (a Spanish player who, at that time, played for an English team) kick the ball from behind the halfway line
5 and score a goal. This kind of goal rarely happens because the halfway line is at least 50 meters away from the goal. That's a long distance to kick a ball!

The next day, Hayward couldn't stop thinking about his **weird** dream. He decided to bet some money on it. He called a friend
10 and bet £200 on his dream. Everyone thought it was a joke.

According to the bet, if Xabi Alonso scored a goal from behind the halfway line in any game that season, Hayward would win £25,000. If he didn't, Hayward would lose £200.

Months passed. Then one afternoon, Hayward was watching a soccer game on TV. Xabi Alonso was playing. At the end of the game, Xabi Alonso had the ball, but he was very far from the net. Then he did something incredible. He kicked the ball 65 meters and scored a goal, just like in Hayward's dream! Alonso's team won the game, and Hayward received £25,000.

It seems some dreams really do come true.

217 words   **Time taken** _____

Reading Comprehension

Choose the correct answers.

1 Hayward's dream _____ .
   a was a nightmare
   b seemed to predict the future
   c was very funny
   d occurred many times

2 What happened in Hayward's dream?
   a He met a famous soccer player.
   b He was a famous soccer player.
   c He saw a soccer player score an unusual goal.
   d He got some money from a famous soccer player.

3 The word **weird** (line 8) means _____ .
   a unimportant
   b funny
   c strange
   d true

4 Why did Hayward call his friend?
   a to ask for some money
   b to repay some money
   c to bet some money
   d to change some money

5 At the end, what happened to Hayward?
   a His friend joined an English soccer team.
   b His team lost a game, and he lost £200.
   c His dream turned into reality, and he won a lot of money.
   d His team won the game, but Hayward didn't get the money.

Vocabulary Index

Unit 1
Chapter 1

area /ˈeriə/ *n.* a place, a location: *The picnic area is near the parking lot.*

buy /baɪ/ *v.* to pay for something: *I buy a newspaper every morning.*

discussion /dɪˈskʌʃən/ *n.* a talk, a serious conversation: *We had a discussion about solving the problem.*

favorite /ˈfeɪvərɪt/ *adj.* most preferred: *Mozart is his favorite composer.*

leave a message /liːv ə ˈmesɪʤ/ *expression* the act of giving a message to someone: *You should leave a message on her voicemail.*

make friends /meɪk frendz/ *expression* to befriend people, the act of socializing and getting to know people: *I usually make a lot of friends at summer camp.*

photo /ˈfoʊtoʊ/ *n.* short for photograph: *I took some photos of my kids.*

send a text message /send ə ˈtekst mesɪʤ/ *expression* to text something to someone, to type a message to be sent: *I used my cell phone to send my mom a text message.*

_____   _____

_____   _____

Chapter 2

connected /kəˈnektɪd/ *adj.* joined together: *The knee bone is connected to the thigh bone.*

crazy /ˈkreɪzi/ *adj.* strange or mentally ill: *People thought they were crazy to try to make money that way.*

like /laɪk/ *adj.* similar to: *The girl is like her mother.*

machine /məˈʃiːn/ something that uses an engine or electricity to do a particular kind of work: *A computer is a machine.*

rock /rɒk/ *n.* a kind of loud music: *Rock music is the best kind of music.*

terrific /təˈrɪf·ɪk/ *adj.* very good: *That was a terrific game. I really liked it.*

tired /taɪərd/ *adj.* sleepy: *I'm so tired.*

turn off /tɜːrn ɒf/ *phr. v.* to stop using: *Please turn off the lights when you leave.*

_____   _____

_____   _____

Unit 2
Chapter 1

at some point /æt səm pɔɪnt/ *phrase* in the future: *At some point you'll have to tell your parents that you failed the test.*

commercial /kəˈmɜːrʃl/ *n.* a radio or television advertisement: *Television programs are often interrupted by commercials.*

continue /kənˈtɪnjuː/ *v.* to carry on for a period of time: *The storm continued for three days.*

graduate /ˈɡrædʒueɪt/ *v.* to receive a degree from an academic institution: *He graduates from high school in June.*

import /ɪmˈpɔːrt/ *v.* to bring products into one country from another: *The jeweler buys diamonds from Africa and imports them into the United States.*

job /dʒɒb/ *n.* work that one is paid to do every day, permanent employment: *She has a good job.*

just about to /dʒʌst əˈbaʊt tə/ *phrase* going to very soon: *I was just about to call you.*

program /ˈproʊɡræm/ *n.* any organized plan to accomplish a goal: *Many government programs help the wealthy.*

_____ _____

_____ _____

Chapter 2

conversation /ˌkɒnvərˈseɪʃn/ *n.* a talk: *I had a conversation about the party with my friend.*

discount /ˈdɪskaʊnt/ *n.* an amount subtracted from a price: *The discount on this item is ten percent off the retail price.*

expensive /ɪkˈspensɪv/ *adj.* costly, high-priced: *He gives expensive gifts to his family for Christmas.*

fast /fæst/ *adv.* rapidly, quickly: *That athlete can run fast.*

outgoing /ˈaʊtˌɡoʊɪŋ/ *adj.* active in seeking the company of others, friendly: *He is an outgoing and lively person.*

poorly /ˈpʊrli/ *adv.* badly: *I did poorly on my math test.*

score /skɔːr/ *n.* a comparison of points between two people or teams: *The final score in the soccer game was 3 to 2.*

shy /ʃaɪ/ *adj.* not liking to talk to people, especially strangers: *The shy boy stood in a dark corner at the dance.*

_____ _____

_____ _____

Unit 3
Chapter 1

after all /ˈæftər ɔːl/ *phrase* everything else having been considered: *We chose to take the train after all.*

encourage /ɪnˈkɜrɪdʒ/ *v.* to inspire (someone) with the courage or confidence (to do something): *My teachers always encouraged us to ask questions.*

enjoy /ɪnˈdʒɔɪ/ *v.* to get pleasure from, to like: *He enjoys music.*

experience /ɪkˈspɪəriəns/ *n.* something that happens which has an effect on you: *I had many great experiences on my trip.*

occupation /ˌɒkjuˈpeɪʃn/ *n.* one's means of making a living, a job: *Her occupation is a doctor.*

promise /ˈprɒmɪs/ *v.* to state to someone that you will certainly do something: *She promised her mother she would come home after school.*

right away /raɪt/ *adv.* immediately, without delay: *When the phone rang, he answered right away.*

set a goal /ɡoʊl/ *expression* to decide to do something: *She set her goals for the year, including getting an A in English.*

_____   _____

_____   _____

Chapter 2

cash /kæʃ/ *n.* paper currency, such as dollar bills, and metal coins used in making daily purchases: *I am going to the bank to get some cash.*

document /ˈdɒkjuːmənt/ *n.* a paper, such as a formal letter, contract, record, etc.: *The official documents showing who owns land are kept in the courthouse.*

earn /ɜːrn/ *v.* to make money by doing work: *I earn about $500 a week.*

expenses /ɪkˈspensəs/ *n.* cost, price: *The expense of moving from one house to another is high.*

project /ˈprɒdʒekt/ *n.* work done for a short time, an assignment: *The project was completed by the entire class in one year.*

skill /skɪl/ *n.* an ability to do something well because of practice, talent, or special training: *She has excellent musical skills.*

tip /tɪp/ *n.* advice, helpful information: *The coach gave a player a tip on how to improve her golf stroke.*

trip /trɪp/ *n.* a journey, travel: *We took a trip north to see our cousin.*

_____   _____

_____   _____

Unit 4
Chapter 1

club /klʌb/ *n.* a group of people who meet because of a common interest: *He belongs to a book club that reads and discusses one book each month.*

compete /kɒmˈpiːt/ *v.* to participate in a contest, to vie: *Our basketball team competed against another team and won.*

originally /əˈrɪdʒənəli/ *adv.* previously, before: *He originally came from Florida but lives in Chicago now.*

point /pɔɪnt/ *n.* a unit of scoring in games: *Our team scored seven points in the first quarter.*

spread /spred/ *v.* to cause something to travel a distance or to many people: *The popularity of comic trading cards spread rapidly throughout Asia.*

team /tiːm/ *n.* two or more people working together, especially in sports: *Our high school football team won the state championship.*

traditional /trəˈdɪʃnl/ *adj.* according to tradition: *She is wearing a traditional dress.*

win /wɪn/ *v.* to score more points than another person or team, to beat: *We win this competition every year.*

_____   _____

_____   _____

Chapter 2

athlete /ˈæθliːt/ *n.* a person who is trained in or has a natural talent for exercises and sports: *He was an outstanding athlete who played several team sports.*

competitive /kɒmˈpətətɪv/ *adj.* liking to compete: *He is very competitive in football; he likes to win.*

divide /dɪˈvaɪd/ *v.* to separate (something into shares): *Divide the candy between the two children.*

event /ɪˈvent/ *n.* a competition, a contest: *I entered the 10K run, an event in which I specialize.*

fan /fæn/ *n.* an admirer: *When the rock star appeared on stage, her fans went wild.*

fight /faɪt/ *v.* to argue, to quarrel: *That couple fights continually over (or about) money.*

parents /ˈperənts/ *n.* the mother and father of someone: *His parents raised him in New Hampshire.*

tourist /ˈtʊrɪst/ *n.* a visitor who travels for pleasure: *Many tourists go to beach and mountain resorts in August.*

_____   _____

_____   _____

Unit 5
Chapter 1

arrive /əˈraɪv/ *v.* to reach a place or destination: *We arrived in town yesterday.*

crowded /ˈkraʊdɪd/ *adj.* full of people, packed: *That subway train is so crowded that no one else can get on.*

incredible /ɪnˈkredəbəl/ *adj.* wonderful: *We had an incredible time on our vacation.*

lunch /lʌntʃ/ *n.* the midday meal: *I have just a sandwich for lunch.*

return /rɪˈtɜːrn/ *v.* to come back, as from a trip: *He returned to his office after lunch in a restaurant.*

souvenir /ˌsuːvəˈnɪr/ *n.* an object bought in order to remember a place: *I bought a little Statue of Liberty as a souvenir of New York City.*

tour /tʊər/ *n.* a series of stops as on a vacation or official trip: *The President made a tour of four capitals in the Middle East.*

view /vjuː/ *n.* a scene: *Our house has a view of the park.*

_____ _____

_____ _____

Chapter 2

chef /ʃef/ *n.* a job, a professional cook: *He's a chef in a famous restaurant.*

dine /daɪn/ *v.* to have dinner: *I enjoy dining in nice restaurants.*

feast /fiːst/ *v.* to eat a lot, to eat a large, special meal: *On his birthday, he invited friends to feast on pizza and ice cream.*

guest /gest/ *n.* a visitor who comes to someone's home for a short time, or to stay for a short time: *We had six guests for dinner last night.*

huge /hjuːdʒ/ *adj.* very large, enormous: *The country suffers from a huge debt.*

impressive /ɪmˈpresɪv/ *adj.* causing someone to feel admiration or respect: *That was an impressive performance. I was amazed.*

relax /rəˈlæks/ *v.* to stop work and enjoy oneself: *She relaxes by riding her bicycle.*

tall /tɔːl/ *adj.* referring to height: *That man is six feet tall.*

_____ _____

_____ _____

Unit 6
Chapter 1

bite /baɪt/ *v.* to use your teeth to cut into something: *You have to teach your children not to bite (other kids).*

custom /ˈkʌstəm/ *n.* a habitual way of behaving that is special to a person, people, region, or nation: *It is his custom to smoke a cigar after dinner.*

host /hoʊst/ *n.* someone who gives a party or has guests: *The meeting is at Sam's house, so he's the host for this week.*

meal /miːl/ *n.* a daily time for eating, known as breakfast, lunch, supper, or dinner, or all the food served at such a time: *Everyone in our family gets together for the evening meal.*

offer /ˈɒfər/ *v.* to propose something, to express willingness to do something: *I offered to take my friend to dinner.*

reach /riːtʃ/ *v.* to stretch out one's arm and hand: *He reached across the table to get the salt.*

rude /ruːd/ *adj.* impolite, making people angry by one's bad behavior or unkind words: *It was rude to walk away while that customer was talking to you.*

take off /teɪk ɒf/ *phr. v.* to remove clothes, disrobe: *He took his clothes off and put on pajamas.*

_____   _____

_____   _____

Chapter 2

confused /kənˈfjuːzd/ *adj.* mixed up mentally so that one cannot understand or think clearly: *He was confused by the teacher's question.*

down /daʊn/ *adj.* in low spirits, depressed: *She's feeling down, so let's try to cheer her up.*

holiday /ˈhɒlədeɪ/ *n.* a day of celebration or rest: *Many companies in the United States give their employees ten legal holidays.*

kind of /kaɪnd əv/ *phrase* a little bit, somewhat: *I am kind of tired; let's go home.*

neighbor /ˈneɪbər/ *n.* person or family that lives next to or near one's house, apartment, etc.: *Our neighbors are very friendly.*

unusual /ʌnˈjuːʒuəl/ *adj.* peculiar, not normal: *His unusual behavior shocks others.*

warm /wɔːrm/ *adj.* kind, friendly: *The hosts gave us a warm welcome.*

weather /ˈweðər/ *n.* the conditions of the sky and air relating to rain, snow, heat, cold, etc.: *In good weather, we go outside.*

_____   _____

_____   _____

Unit 7
Chapter 1

child /tʃaɪld/ *n.* a very young person, who is no longer a baby but not yet an adolescent: *The couple's youngest child is three years old.*

control /kənˈtroʊl/ *v.* to have power or authority: *Mr. Shin controls the company, but he cannot control his anger.*

describe /dɪˈskraɪb/ *v.* to tell what something looks like, to report: *The reporter described the event as it was happening.*

go out /goʊ aʊt/ *phr. v.* to spend time with someone: *I like going out with my friends.*

grow up /groʊ ʌp/ *phr. v.* to mature: *Our daughter has grown up now.*

protect /prəˈtekt/ *v.* to defend against harm or loss: *She protected her face from the sun with a hat.*

rule /ruːl/ *n.* a statement about what must or should be done: *Our school has a rule that students must not eat or drink in class.*

strict /strɪkt/ *adj.* expecting rules to be followed, requiring obedience: *The strict teacher makes us stay after school if we don't do our homework.*

_____   _____

_____   _____

Chapter 2

care about /ˈkeər əbaʊt/ *phr. v.* If you care about something, it is important to you.: *That company says they care about the environment.*

childish /ˈtʃaɪldɪʃ/ *adj.* unreasonable, failing to be adult, immature: *Oh, don't be so childish! Take your medicine.*

crowd /kraʊd/ *n.* a large number of persons gathered together: *Before the store opened, there was a huge crowd of people waiting outside.*

frown /fraʊn/ *v.* to have an expression of anger, disapproval, or worry on one's face: *She frowned when she heard the bad news.*

make fun of /meɪk fʌn əv/ *phr. v.* to ridicule, tease someone: *Comedians like to make fun of politicians.*

outsider /ˌaʊtˈsaɪdər/ *n.* a person not thought of as a member of a group, a stranger: *People in that small town avoid talking to outsiders.*

pressure /ˈpreʃər/ *n.* a feeling of being pushed to do things: *The pressure of meeting deadlines in her job causes her to sleep poorly.*

put on /pʊt ɒn/ *phr. v.* to wear: *You put on a hat on a sunny day.*

_____   _____

_____   _____

Unit 8
Chapter 1

afraid /əˈfreɪd/ *adj.* fearful: *The child is afraid of dogs.*

brave /breɪv/ *adj.* unafraid of danger: *Firefighters are brave in saving people from burning buildings.*

climb /klaɪm/ *v.* to move upward: *The airplane took off and climbed above the clouds.*

fear /fɪər/ *n.* a strong feeling of fright about danger (harm, trouble, etc.): *The hunter was filled with fear when he saw the bear running toward him.*

give up /gɪv ʌp/ *v.* to stop doing something: *I gave up smoking last year.*

look for /lʊk fər/ *phr. v.* to search, to seek: *The child looked for his missing ball.*

native /ˈneɪtɪv/ *n.* a person from a certain place such as a country: *Greg went to college in Australia but is a native of New Zealand.*

reach /riːtʃ/ *v.* to arrive at a place: *It took three days for the climbers to reach the top of the mountain.*

_____   _____

_____   _____

Chapter 2

challenge /ˈtʃælɪndʒ/ *n.* a difficult job: *She found her new sales job to be quite a challenge.*

deliver /dɪˈlɪvər/ *v.* to take goods to a place of business, a home, etc.: *Trucks deliver food to supermarkets.*

distance /ˈdɪstəns/ *n.* amount of space between two points: *What is the distance between the Earth and the moon?*

make a mistake /mɪˈsteɪk/ *expression* to do something wrong: *She made a mistake at work and made her boss very angry.*

option /ˈɒpʃn/ *n.* choice, an alternative: *She has two options: she can stay here or leave.*

organized /ˈɔːrgənaɪzd/ *adj.* tidy, neat: *Mary is very efficient and organized in everything that she does.*

pick up /pɪk ʌp/ *phr. v.* to go and get something: *He picked up a pizza on his way home.*

system /ˈsɪstəm/ *n.* an ordered, logical set of ideas: *He has a system for everything.*

_____   _____

_____   _____

Unit 9
Chapter 1

compliment /ˈkɒmpləmənt/ *v.* something nice you say about someone: *Jay gave her a compliment yesterday when he said her dress was nice.*

current /ˈkʌrənt/ *adj.* happening now: *In current events, the president is making a speech about the new laws.*

exchange /ɪksˈtʃeɪndʒ/ *v.* to give something and get something back, to trade: *At lunch today, I exchanged my sandwich for Mike's pasta.*

expression /ɪkˈspreʃn/ *n.* a group of words, a statement, an idiom: *When you tell someone to "break a leg," it is just an expression meaning "good luck."*

film /fɪlm/ *n.* a movie, a motion picture: *The movie theaters on Broadway show the latest films.*

perform /pərˈfɔːrm/ *v.* to act in front of people: *The actors performed a play for the queen.*

poetry /ˈpoʊətri/ *n.* a written and oral literary form composed in verse, poems in general: *Poetry has been composed since ancient times.*

role /roʊl/ *n.* a part played by an actor or actress: *She plays the leading role in a television show.*

_____   _____

_____   _____

Chapter 2

create /kriˈeɪt/ *v.* to make something in a special way, with skill or artistry: *That company created a new product.*

flexible /ˈfleksɪbl/ *adj.* can bend easily without breaking: *She's really flexible! She can bend her legs over her head.*

graceful /ˈɡreɪsfəl/ *adj.* moving in a smooth, relaxed, and attractive way, or having a smooth, attractive shape: *A swan is a very graceful animal. Look how it glides smoothly on the water.*

lift /lɪft/ *v.* to carry something or someone, and put it/them in a higher position: *He lifted the box onto the table.*

live /laɪv/ *adj.* not recorded, an actual performance: *I like watching live bands.*

original /əˈrɪdʒənəl/ *adj.* special and interesting because of not being the same as others: *That piece of art is really original. I've never seen anything like it.*

performance /pərˈfɔːrməns/ *n.* an event in which people perform a play, a piece of music, a dance, etc.: *I bought two tickets to tonight's performance of* Swan Lake.

stage /steɪdʒ/ *n.* the raised area in a theatre where actors perform: *For our school play, we had to fit the whole class on the stage in the hall.*

_____   _____

_____   _____

Unit 10
Chapter 1

dress /dres ʌp/ *v.* to wear clothes: *Daisy dressed in her nicest outfit to attend the wedding.*

fashion /ˈfæʃn/ *n.* any style of dress popular for a period of time: *It used to be the fashion for women to wear gloves when they went out.*

pay attention /peɪ əˈtenʃən/ *expression* to watch, listen to, or think about something carefully or with interest: *You weren't paying attention to what I was saying.*

report /rɪˈpɔːt/ *v.* to describe a recent event or situation: *She reported that the situation had changed.*

runway /ˈrʌnweɪ/ *n.* a narrow platform extending from the stage into the audience in a theater or nightclub: *During the fashion show, the models walked smoothly down the runway.*

simply /ˈsɪmpli/ *adv.* just; only: *I simply don't trust him.*

snap a picture /snæp ə ˈpɪktʃər/ *expression v.* take a photo: *Sean carries his camera everywhere so he can snap a picture of anything he likes.*

style /staɪl/ *n.* a way of designing hair, clothes, furniture, etc: *She had her hair cut in a really nice style.*

_____   _____

_____   _____

Chapter 2

admit /ədˈmɪt/ *v.* to agree that you did something, or that something, usually bad, is true: *He admitted that he had stolen the money.*

come up with /kʌm ʌp wɪð/ *phr. v.* to be the first person to think of something, to invent something: *It was Dr Andy Hildebrand who came up with the idea for the voice pitch-correcting software called Auto-Tune.*

designer /dɪˈzaɪnər/ *n.* someone who draws and plans how something will be made: *That bag was created by a very famous designer.*

made out of /meɪk aʊt əv/ *phrase* When something is made out of something else, it is built or put together using that material.: *That house is special because the walls are made out of plants.*

recycle /ˌriːˈsaɪkl/ *v.* to put used paper, glass, plastic, etc. through a process so that it can be used again: *We should always recycle paper.*

remind /rɪˈmaɪnd/ *v.* to make someone remember something, or remember to do something: *Can you please remind me to call my dad?*

take care of /teɪk keər əv/ *phr. v.* to take charge of the maintenance, support, or treatment of something or someone: *She promised to take care of the new puppy.*

weird /wɪrd/ *adj.* odd, bizarre: *Sometimes we hear weird noises that sound like crying in the night.*

_____   _____

_____   _____

Unit 11
Chapter 1

a number of /ə ˈnʌmbər əv/ *phrase* several: *She gave me a number of suggestions.*

author /ˈɔːθəʳ/ *n.* someone who writes a book, article, etc.: *J. K. Rowling is a well-known author.*

discover /dɪˈskʌvər/ *v.* to find, to see, or to learn of (something no one knew before): *Galileo discovered the planet Jupiter.*

expert /ˈekspɜːt/ *n.* someone who has a lot of skill in something or a lot of knowledge about something: *He's an expert on ancient cultures.*

full of /fʊl əv/ *phrase.* containing a lot of things or people or a lot of something: *The jar was full of cookies.*

handwritten /hændˈrɪtən/ *adj.* written with a pen or pencil, not typed: *He sent me a handwritten note.*

mean /miːn/ *v.* to have a particular meaning, to intend to express a fact or opinion: *That word means "hello."*

mysterious /mɪˈstɪriəs/ *adj.* strange, not known or not understood: *No one knows where he disappeared to. It's all very mysterious.*

_____   _____

_____   _____

Chapter 2

case /keɪs/ *n.* a particular situation or example of something, or a crime that police are trying to solve: *Over the last year, there have been many cases of burglary in this area.*

curious /ˈkjʊəriəs/ *adj.* something strange or unusual: *The house was decorated in a curious style.*

demand /dɪˈmænd/ *v.* to ask for something in a way that shows that you do not expect to be refused: *My mother demanded I help her with the housework.*

flight /flaɪt/ *n.* a journey in an aircraft: *The flight to Japan took four hours.*

give instructions /gɪv ɪnˈstrʌkʃənz / *v.* to tell someone to do something, to give someone information that explains how to do or use something: *He gave the students instructions to finish their homework that day.*

passenger /ˈpæsəndʒəʳ/ *n.* someone who is travelling in a vehicle, but not controlling the vehicle: *There were four people in the car—the driver and three passengers.*

take off /teɪk ɒf/ *v.* action done by a plane when it goes into the air: *Please turn off your cell phone while the plane takes off.*

worry /ˈwʌri/ *v.* to think about problems or unpleasant things that might happen in a way that makes you feel anxious: *It worried him when she didn't come home on time.*

_____   _____

_____   _____

Unit 12
Chapter 1

believe /bɪˈliːv/ *v.* to be convinced of something, to know or feel that an idea, situation, or way of behaving is true: *She believed her son when he said he didn't start the fight.*

find out /faɪnd aʊt/ *v.* to learn: *I just found out there is a test tomorrow.*

nightmare /ˈnaɪtmeər/ *n.* a frightening dream: *The poor child had a nightmare.*

noise /nɔɪz/ *n.* a sound, especially an unpleasant one: *We heard a strange noise.*

real /ˈriːəl/ *adj.* true, not fake or imaginary: *His real name is Bob Smith, not John Jones.*

run away /rʌn əˈweɪ/ *phr. v.* to leave: *My cat ran away last night.*

scream /skriːm/ *v.* to cry out with a high, loud voice in pain or fear: *He screamed for help.*

stand up /stænd ʌp/ *phr. v.* to get on one's feet: *He was sitting, then he stood up.*

_____ _____

_____ _____

Chapter 2

accident /ˈæksɪdənt/ *n.* something bad which happens that is not intended and which causes injury or damage: *I didn't mean to push him. It was an accident.*

celebrate /ˈseləbreɪt/ *v.* to do something enjoyable because it is a special day, or because something good has happened: *Do you celebrate Chinese New Year?*

elevator /ˈelɪveɪtər/ *n.* a machine that carries people up and down in tall buildings: *We took the elevator to the 12th floor.*

rescue /ˈreskjuː/ *v.* to save or free someone from a dangerous or unpleasant situation: *Firefighters rescued the child from the burning building.*

survive /səˈvaɪv/ *v.* to continue to live after almost dying because of an accident, illness, etc.: *No one survived the plane crash.*

tool /tuːl/ *n.* something that helps you to do a particular activity: *I find the best tool for that activity is a hammer.*

trapped /træpt/ *adj.* unable to move or escape from a place or situation: *They were trapped by the fire. There was no way out.*

terrifying /ˈterɪfaɪɪŋ/ *adj.* scary, horrifying, fearful: *It was a terrifying moment when the bank robber pointed his gun at me.*

_____ _____

_____ _____

Prefixes and Suffixes

Here is a list of prefixes and suffixes that appear in the reading passages of this book.

Prefix	Meaning	Example
bi	two	bicycle
in, im	related to inside or inwards	income, import
inter	between two or more places or groups	Internet, international
kilo	a thousand	kilometer
mid	referring to the middle	midnight, midday
re	back, again	return, reheat, resend
tele	far	television, telephone
un	not, negative	unkind, unknown, unpack
uni	one	university, united
well-	done well or a lot	well-known, well-understood

Suffix	Meaning	Example
able	full of	comfortable, enjoyable, remarkable
al	used to make an adjective from a noun	national, informal, personal
an, ian	relating to	American, Canadian, Australian
ant	one who does something	flight attendant
ant/ent	indicating an adjective	important, independent
ation/ution/ition	used to make a noun from a verb	information, preparation
ence	added to some adjectives to make a noun	independence
ent	used to make an adjective from a verb	excellent
ent	one who does something	student
er, or	someone or something that does something	singer, dancer, writer
er	(after an adjective) more	faster, safer
ese	relating to	Japanese, Chinese
est	(after an adjective) most	closest, earliest, thinnest
ful	filled with	helpful, careful
hood	state or condition	childhood, livelihood
ion, sion, tion	indicating a noun	comprehension, discussion

Reading Rate Chart

Time (minutes)	Review Reading								Rate (words per minute)
	1	2	3	4	5	6	7	8	
1:00									200
1:15									160
1:30									133
1:45									114
2:00									100
2:15									88
2:30									80
2:45									72
3:00									66
3:15									61
3:30									57
3:45									53
4:00									50
4:15									47
4:30									44
4:45									42
5:00									40
5:15									38
5:30									36
5:45									34
6:00									33
6:15									32
6:30									30
6:45									29
7:00									28

Reading Comprehension Chart

Score	Review Reading							
	1	2	3	4	5	6	7	8
5								
4								
3								
2								
1								
0								